THE *Gospel*

ACCORDING TO

IMPROV

A Radical Way
OF CREATIVE AND SPONTANEOUS
LIVING

Les Carpenter

 Morehouse Publis
NEW YORK

Morehouse Publishing, 19 East 34th Street, New York, NY 10016

Morehouse Publishing is an imprint of Church Publishing Incorporated.

Cover design by Marc Whitaker, MTWdesign
Typeset by PerfecType, Nashville, Tennessee

Library of Congress Cataloging-in-Publication Data
Names: Carpenter, Les (Reverend), author.
Title: The gospel according to improv : a radical way of creative and spontaneous living / Les Carpenter.
Description: New York, NY : Morehouse Publishing, [2022]
Identifiers: LCCN 2021047515 (print) | LCCN 2021047516 (ebook) | ISBN 9781640653634 (paperback) | ISBN 9781640653641 (ebook)
Subjects: LCSH: Christian life. | Pastoral theology. | Improvisation (Acting) | Spontaneity (Personality trait) | Meaning (Philosophy)--Religious aspects--Christianity.
Classification: LCC BV4501.3 .C264 2022 (print) | LCC BV4501.3 (ebook) | DDC 248.4--dc23/eng/20211118
LC record available at https://lccn.loc.gov/2021047515
LC ebook record available at https://lccn.loc.gov/2021047516

Dedicated to all the soul-friends who helped me
see brilliance and beauty both on and off the stage.

"[Love] does not insist on its own way."

—1 Corinthians 13:5

CONTENTS

vii

INTRODUCTION

When I was in high school, I went to a youth ministry retreat for six days. I was delighted and elated to meet people that seemed to find me interesting. As a teen it felt miraculous to find a group of peers who enthusiastically and unconditionally welcomed me just for showing up. Near the end of the week, the leaders asked for volunteers to help plan our closing communion service. They told us the bishop would be there, and they wanted the youth to be involved in the planning. By "involved," what they meant was they put us in a room with a bunch of prayer books and said, "Go."

I became deeply aware that while we were trying our best, none of us actually knew what we were doing. Still, we made the best of it. People started volunteering for different jobs in the service. Three people wanted to do readings, so we figured one would do the Hebrew Bible reading, one could do the New Testament reading, and one could do the Gospel reading. However, none of us realized there was a rule buried in the rubrics of that pair of prayer books that said only someone who is ordained can do the Gospel reading. It wasn't until after we had finished our preparations that I learned about this rule, and it scared me. I didn't want to offend the bishop or the adults that trusted us to do it "right."

I didn't dare ask about the issue and didn't know what was going to happen until we were in the middle of the service. As is common in the Episcopal Church, there was a Gospel procession where the cross, torchbearers, and a Gospel book are processed out into the middle of the congregation. We like this ritual because it puts the story of the Gospel in the middle of the people. I was curious when I noticed that

1

both the young woman who had volunteered to read the Gospel and the deacon were in the procession. A deacon is the ordained person who ordinarily reads the Gospel. As we continued to sing, I wondered what would happen. The young woman stood in front of the open Gospel Book, and the deacon unpinned his stole and laid it over her shoulder as she proclaimed the Gospel.

I've told this story in churches before, and every time I tell it there is an audible gasp. I used to wonder if that gasp was because those who heard the story were offended or because they were moved. Over time I have realized it was the latter. A deacon was present during one of those sermons and blurted out "No he didn't!" when I told the story—but it wasn't out of offense. It was out of awe because moments like that show us the Gospel. Much later I learned that there is a technical term for what happened that day. It is called "Yes, &" or "overacceptance." "Yes, &" is the basis of improv comedy, and the more that I master this practice, the closer I get to touching the inconceivable mystery that is God's grace.

I have had no experience in church or on stage that defines my understanding of the priesthood or even my Christian faith better than that moment with the deacon and the young woman. I, too, am in awe of it. Extending the stole is what I try to do every day, and I know this is what God does for each and every one of us.

I knew I was watching something beautiful that day, but I didn't understand what it felt like to live inside of moments like that. Eventually I dedicated my life to the study of the same God that young woman was proclaiming. Just like music, family, love, and all the other best things in life, these moments can't really be understood from the outside. Appreciated, yes, but not understood. Finding improv comedy gave me not only the release I needed to survive the priesthood but also a mechanism for understanding how to put into practice the experience that I've been talking about ever since that day.

I often wonder about that angelic soul who had the thought, "Hey, we could both respect the deacon's authority and empower this young person." For years I used to wonder how someone came up with that kind of graceful creativity. Now I know: practice.

Other pastors and authors have talked about improv. While there are some glaring exceptions, most seem to me to use improv as a means to illustrate what they already thought. This book is not that. The practice of improv saved my priesthood, integrated my mind and soul, and finally taught me to make visceral sense out of what I learned about God in church and seminary. The awkward, scary, thrilling, and hilarious lessons of improv have become a bridge between what Christians talk about and how we live. Those lessons challenge and strengthen me in every conversation I have, or even in each breath I take. They are a gift to me every day, and now I give them to you.

Reading This Book Won't Work

When you are both a priest and an improviser, the word gets out quick. I am often invited to speak or share on improv and the gospel. I am not a known name in the Church, so usually I am offered the church conference equivalent of an opening act. They give me a quick slot in the beginning because the organizers don't want the participants to feel bored, and they figure at least I will be funny. While I deeply appreciate the gig, I always chuckle inside because it is clear that they don't know me or what this improv stuff is about.

Improvisation isn't about "being funny," which is good because I am not. My humor is an acquired taste, like coffee, or whiskey, or gasoline. I mean, I can go off on puns all day long, because it is funny to me to watch how not funny they are to those around me, but the skills and philosophy of improvisation (and the gospel for that matter) are not about trying to achieve a result. They are a *process* that reveals the humor, the creativity, the beauty, and the grace in this life we live.

Whenever I am invited to speak, I ask if there will be space for me to get participants to actually improvise with each other as part of my presentation. A predictable dead silence follows on the phone because the organizer is thinking, "Wait, this was supposed to be the 'fun' thing, and that sounds scary. People aren't going to want to do something where they will fail." Then there is this awkward back-and-forth with me and the organizer where they try to imagine why I would ask such a crazy thing, and lobby me to do something fun or funny instead. Then I tell them the truest thing I know about improv. **Watching improv is entertaining (well, hopefully), but doing improv is transformative.**

A few years ago the word "neuroplasticity" was in vogue. I remember once hearing four different people say it in the course of one day, which surprised me because I don't usually spend time with people who will spend more than three syllables on a word. Basically, the idea of neuroplasticity is that your brain rewires itself. It is not just that you can be exposed to a new thought; with practice you can create a whole new way of thinking. This is extremely useful in the case of brain injury, but it also has huge implications for how we experience the world. Changing what we think can change the way we think. We can learn peace, joy, patience, and generosity. We can learn to be more creative, or holy, or even funnier—but only through practice.

Let that seep in for a moment. When I sit with that idea, I also hear an echo of some of Jesus's words. "Your faith has made you well" (Matt. 9:22). It is the faith that changes the reality.

Here is my recommendation. Take an improv class while you read this book. Heck, take twelve. Short of that, I am providing a list of exercises you can do as you read this book. Understanding these ideas can make for a fun read, but improv has changed my faith and my ministry, not because of my understanding, but because of the gifts that came when I experimented with these methods of graceful living. I learned that **there is one way to becoming more creative and loving: act that way as much as possible**. Hopefully this book will help you reflect on these practices and give you some ideas about how you can do just that. In the end, though, only you, with God's help, can rewire your brain. As my friend the Rev. Gini Gerbasi said in my all-time favorite last line of a sermon, "Good luck with that."

SECTION

"Yes, &"—Collaboration,
Creativity, Incarnation,
and Salvation

Chapter 1

The First Class

Embracing the Awkward

L et's face it: life is awkward. From first breath to the first day of school, from first dates to last rites, most of us try to escape awkwardness as if we were hiding in the shade from the Texas summer sun. Between awkward moments, we struggle with the overwhelming desire to find meaning. How do we love well, stay authentic, build community, enjoy life, and live justly all at the same time? No one knows, but sheer probability implies the gifts of awkwardness play a huge role.

I don't claim to be an expert on life, or improv, or even faith. It cracks me up every time I see my seminary degree listed as "master of divinity," as if God's ways are something you could master. More than that, though, I think you will find in these pages that I am not particularly courageous, smart, or wise—but that is the good news. I am aware that my ordained ministry was set up to fail. Maybe all of them are. But after a dozen years I am still kicking along, loving my people deeply, witnessing miracles, and having fun because of one very simple thing: God led me to the practices of improv early in my ministry and those practices have become so ingrained in my understanding of life and work that I literally cannot pull them apart.

The burnout rate among clergy, much less laypeople serious about ministry, is through the roof. When I think about my ministry, I am reminded of Paul's constant badgering of his own church plant in 1 Corinthians: "The world thought you all were idiots. That is why God chose you. If losers like you can do this love and ministry stuff, then God must be phenomenal."[1]

Some of these improv/Gospel lessons will make sense. Others will seem ridiculous. I encourage you to open your mind, body, and soul and try them. Don't be afraid to read aloud or shout. In fact, I dare you to right now let out a big "Yippee!" Getting used to embracing that awkward feeling in your body is the beginning of inspiration and joy. Every improviser knows this truth because we have in common the experience of going to our first improv class. One thing is sure: it was excruciating.

Prologue to My First Class

I have a lot of practice in being awkward. Ask anyone in my middle school about the phase where I wore a hat with a fish through it every day. Still, nothing had prepared me for that brisk night on Massachusetts Avenue in Indianapolis.

It was a bizarre and painful confluence of events in my life that brought me there. I had been a priest less than a year and I wasn't sure if I would make it to year two. Many people have a rough time learning how to be a priest and I was no different. I am sure the same is true for many careers, but to become a priest in the Episcopal Church you must convince a group of strangers that it is who you truly are. They call it the "ontological priesthood," and while we believe that all people have a calling from God that will bring them challenge and fulfillment, I know of no other calling that expects you to bare your soul, say, "This is who I am," and then wait (often for years) for

---

1. 1 Corinthians 1:26–28. Loosely translated.

people you don't know to say, "Sure," or, "Nah." I will point out that for any other job we would say that this thinking is unhealthy. Can you imagine someone at a psychiatrist's office saying, "No, Doc, you don't understand. Being an accountant is who I am. It is who I am meant to be. I am nothing without debits or credits. I am failing as a human being unless I can be an agent of reconciliation." That person would leave with some serious prescriptions. Yet we require clergy to talk that way not just in front of psychiatrists (there is extensive psychological testing to become a priest in our church), but also in what is basically a job interview. I shouldn't complain because I don't have a better idea for how to discern who is right for this work, and there is no question to me that faith, ministry, and the priesthood make their way into your identity, but I also have come to believe that having some critical distance from that process is invaluable. What I didn't know when I walked into that black box theater is that the one thing I needed to learn how to do was to separate my vocation—my calling—from my job.[2]

I had a lot on the line with this priest thing, and after less than a year, it was shaky at best. I found what on paper should have been the best job in the Episcopal Church. I was just a hair under thirty when I was ordained, and I was hired to work in a gorgeous church doing young adult ministry (for people in their twenties and thirties). At the time the average age of Americans was thirty-three and the average age of an Episcopalian was sixty-three. That's right, at just about thirty, I was the difference. And the difference was a priest.

Not long after my ordination my boss, the rector (head pastor), was removed from his position because he had had an affair. Many people were hurt and angry. The church had suffered from similar situations in the past. Then the other priest on staff had to take a leave of absence to care for her husband, who was dying of Alzheimer's. With less than a month's experience as a priest, I was the only one

2. In my experience that is the only way to do both well.

left standing in this large church (350+ people on average per Sunday) with an endowment of over $30 million. Oh—did I mention the stock market had crashed and the church had laid off a bunch of employees right before the rector was removed?

That's when I realized that the ontological priesthood had gotten the better of me. All I thought about was what was going on at the church. I was trying to reach out to a completely different group of people and bring them into this institution that was shaken and bitter and weak. While there was a lot about my situation that was unique, I didn't realize that trying to reach out to a completely different group of people and bring them into an institution that was shaken and bitter and weak was what most clergy and vestries (board of directors of an Episcopal church) do most of the time.

I am not sure how the next thing dawned on me. Sometimes I joke that the clouds opened up and I heard a great voice, but, somehow, I came to the conclusion that I needed a hobby. I needed friends that weren't wrapped up in this system. I needed a social outlet. I needed something to do to escape from the world of church. It is ironic that my escape would open up a world of seeing and doing that would breathe life (Gen. 2:7) into the priesthood I was hiding from. Why improv? I figured I didn't have time to pick something that would take preparation. I was so ignorant. It's funny. Sometimes I miss naive Les.

The First Class

I was crazy scared. I have always been shy, and my stage fright is off the charts, which is yet another little irony of my preacher/improviser life. Between seminary and my parish ministry, I hadn't met anyone in about four years who didn't know anything about my religious preferences. The point was to get my head out of church. I decided that I would keep that part of my life quiet for as long as reasonably possible. Admitting you are a priest to a group of strangers is a bit like passing gas in an elevator. No one says anything and everyone backs away slowly.

We began the class by sitting in a circle in a well-worn black box theater room in the middle of Indianapolis. I twisted nervously in the squeaky folding chair, feeling far from the protections of the pulpit, much less suburbia. I hadn't ventured into public in a T-shirt since my ordination, and here I was with people who had no idea who I was. I thought it would feel liberating. Instead, it felt like just a matter of time until my secret came out.

We were almost halfway through the introductions, and I was wound so tight I hadn't listened to a single name or detail.

"What about you? What's your name, what do you do?" The teacher's raspy voice sailed toward a particularly scruffy-looking individual across the circle.

"I am Larry, and I am . . ." Larry looked around slyly with his big brown, golden shepherd eyes, ". . . and I am a contract killer." He seemed to be waiting for a laugh, but none came.

"No," said the teacher. "First rule of this class. Don't try to be funny."

Internally, I panicked a little; judging by the confused and desperate looks around the circle, I wasn't the only one. No one made a squeak, but the sound of our collective thought was deafening.

How are we supposed to learn improv comedy without trying to be funny? we all wondered together.

"Uhhh," said Larry.

"What do you do for real?" asked the teacher.

"I'm a cook," Larry said, looking down.

The guy next to him chimed in, "So I was going to say that I am a priest, but since we aren't supposed to be funny . . ."

"Yep," said the teacher.

"My name is Winston. I teach middle school," the guy said.

I was next in line. "My name is Les—and this is awkward, but I am actually an Episcopal priest." I was so embarrassed that I couldn't look any of my classmates in the face. Then I heard the teacher's voice. It sounded uncharacteristically soft and kind.

"Okay. That's good."

That was probably a huge mistake, I thought to myself, *but at least I know that my teacher is a good actor.*

Les's First Rule of Improv and Spirituality

I don't tell this story so that you can feel sorry for me. I hope this story doesn't scare you away from improv class. That was the beginning of one of the greatest blessings of my life. I will point out that almost all of us came back for the next class and most of us fell in love with the art form. I tell the story because it reveals something about the nature of the experience of doing improv.

The emotional response that I call awkwardness is what improvisers refer to as being "in your head." You are in your head when you are so focused on how things look or how bad or good you are doing that you stop being fully in the moment. Most of us know the crushing self-critical voice, and most of us know those demon whispers that keep us from finding creativity, love, and meaning. Almost all the teachings of improv are strategies that help you get out of your head and into something more interesting, like the moment, or your body, or your connection with your partner. As you work on those strategies, they go from being a method to a set of choices, and then from a set of choices to an instinct, which allows them to be there in real time. Eventually you come to love the awkward moments because of the potential they offer.

You can see the love of awkward in the comedy we create. Watch any movie from one of our generation's great improvisers: Tina Fey, Amy Poehler, Mike Birbiglia, Kristen Wiig. The force behind all their strongest comedic moments is awkwardness. They are hilarious *because* they have mastered the awkward feeling that we all get.

Many people have written and taught about the "rules of improv," which you will hear more about in the rest of this book. People especially talk about "Yes, &" as the foundation of all improv, but I will submit "Embrace the awkward" as an unwritten rule that is even more foundational both to good improv and to the gospel of Jesus Christ.

From an improv perspective, this is evidenced by the first class. Long before we learned anything about what to do, we were all cowering and afraid to be seen. I can't tell you how many evenings I sat in the bar next to that improv theater with those same people, laughing and joking and retelling what that first night was like from each of our tortured perspectives.

Awkwardness is the prelude to meaning. It is that push of resistance that tries to keep your true, beloved self hidden from view. **Awkwardness is the doorway to grace, because awkwardness is the sensation we feel when we realize that we are losing control.** Without the ability to push through those moments, there are laughs, but no belly laughs. There is fun, but there is no full joy.[3] We are trained by our society to value control and so we choose comfort and predictability over awkwardness, but in my experience that leaves us in the shallow end of the pool of life.

A New Dimension in Seeing

I imagine that many of you are thinking, "I see your point about improv, but what does that have to do with Jesus?" Well, Jesus's ministry was ridiculously awkward. I mean, what kind of teacher speaks in parables and riddles with the express purpose of being misunderstood?[4] What kind of miracle worker heals someone only

---

3. Cf. John 15:11
4. Matthew 13:13

to tell them not to tell anyone about it?[5] What kind of anointed king tells people to hide his identity?[6] Or to get serious, let's look at Jesus's greatest hits for a second. The parable of the good Samaritan is generally taught in Sunday school as a lovely story on the importance of charity. Ask most church-going Americans what a Samaritan is and they will say it is a good person. But Jesus told the parable to people who hated Samaritans. Samaritans were seen as religious half-breeds. To tell a story where a Samaritan was seen as your neighbor, much less to make him the hero of the story, was akin to opening a speech at a MAGA protest with a story about how patriotic Bernie Sanders is. Because of his consistent teachings, Jesus was so awkward and inflammatory that everyone in power wanted him dead.

Sorry. That got heavy. The crucifixion usually does. What I am suggesting is that we stop looking at Jesus's halo and start looking at his pedagogical style and his manner of life. He was the misfit rabbi of a bunch of quirky reject students. Even as he prodded and mocked those in power, he did it in surprisingly playful ways. Love is always awkward.

The Bible tells us that "God is love,"[7] and through love Jesus shows us the loving way, which is great, yet when we look at his way of being, we realize that it is one misadventure after another. His mother guilts him into his first miracle to save a wedding reception; his own disciples don't understand what he is doing half the time. **This strange awkwardness is the most dominant theme in Jesus's ministry, and I believe it is the key to knowing him.** The issue is that we bind the Gospel in a golden book and read it out loud with our best James Earl Jones impression. When we don't like the awkwardness, we delete it from the way we tell the story. We treat it as if it were perfect and beautiful, effortless and graceful. But Jesus is the guy who

---

5. E.g., Mark 1:43–45
6. E.g., Mark 8:29–30
7. 1 John 4:16

gets in between Martha and Mary's sibling issues. He is the guy proclaimed the Messiah by a bug-eating desert dweller. Even the Pharisee Nicodemus had the good sense to sneak in and talk to Jesus at night so his curiosity could be concealed from his colleagues. **Jesus ups the game on love, which means he also ups the game on awkward**.

Love is awkward. Loving your enemies even more so. I cannot imagine a moment more beautiful and awkward than when Jesus said, "Father, forgive them; for they do not know what they are doing" (Luke 23:34).

Awkward Conversation Exercise

Embracing the awkward is a spiritual practice, so it takes actual practice. You can't learn how to pray by reading a book. You have to actually pray if you want to draw closer to the divine. Everything I am talking about in this book is a series of practices, inspired and informed by theatrical improvisation and designed to increase our ease at living, leading, and creating in Christian ways.

I will be honest. When I read a book that has practical application sections, I skip them. If that is what you are going to do, I can't stop you. But I will say this: if there is ever a book to pay attention to the exercise sections, this is the one. As I said before, watching improv is entertaining, but doing improv is transformative. These exercises are designed to be playful breaks that solidify the ideas of the book as you start to rework your brain's thinking in ways that enrich the soul.

- Take a breath and prepare yourself to experience and savor this exercise.
- Think of someone you know who makes you feel awkward.
- I am betting it didn't take long for you to think of that person.
- Imagine them in your mind. Maybe you naturally laugh at them. Maybe they drive you crazy.

- Try to remember what they sound like. Try to remember how they hold their body. Picture in your mind the way that they walk.
- Ok, get up and begin to walk like that. Try to feel in your body what it feels like to inhabit their character. Feel free to lovingly exaggerate some of their characteristics.
- Try to make vocal sounds that sound like them. Do they have a catchphrase or just a line that you remember them saying? Try to say it in the best impression you have.
- Let yourself begin to enjoy soaking into that character. Even if you find them frustrating in real life, accept that you can watch them on this imaginary plane and they cannot hurt you or anyone else. Try to focus on their quirks that are unrelated to any conflict you might have with them.
- Keep this up until you find an authentic chuckle of amused appreciation about the person. If you run out of time before you can find that, know that you can always come back to this exercise later, or start again with a different person.

What I have just walked you through is the start of developing an impression of a person. I say "impression" like you would see on *Saturday Night Live* or another comedy sketch show. Impressions are often misunderstood. Often the audience wants to laugh at the subject of the impression. They get that feeling of perverse glee we know from the schoolyard where we mocked the little guy to feel big inside. That is not an impression. Impressions take fair hits at their target, but the performer needs to be careful. If you get mean-spirited, it stops being funny fast.

During the run-up to the 2016 presidential election, there was a lot of mean-spirited rhetoric on Twitter between President Donald Trump and comedian Rosie O'Donnell. *Saturday Night Live* has made a living off of impressions of political figures since its beginning. A lot of folks on social media wanted to see Rosie O'Donnell play Steve Bannon, one of President Trump's top advisors. Lorne Michaels, *SNL*'s creator and producer, reportedly told a cast member why he passed on the idea of Ms. O'Donnell playing Bannon: "When you're playing a character, you can't play it from hate. You have to play it from funny, because when you play it from hate, it looks like you're just being mean."[8]

I'll confess that I am not much of an impressionist, but my intuition tells me that the truth goes even further than Lorne's quote. When you truly inhabit another person's point of view, even from a perspective of jest, the consequence is empathy. From a Christian perspective, if you want an impression of someone to be hilarious, you have to find a way to love them at least a little for the broken, quirky person they are.

Whenever I am gearing up for a difficult conversation with someone in ministry, whether it is someone not doing their job or passing rumors or whatever, I do this exercise in my office. I try to find their character physically because, at least in my experience, empathy rarely can take root in the mind before it has taken root in the body. •

Don't Try to Be Funny. Don't Try to Be Righteous

One of the things that sat strange for me from that first class, and I think for all the other students too, was when the teacher told us not to try to be funny. How could we do something without trying? Once again it gets back to control. I have since come to believe my teacher was 100 percent right.

The enemy of humor is "trying to be funny." Humor is about being in the wonder of the moment. Humor is about being alive enough to let go and delight in what is happening now. You can't

8. Joanna Robinson, "*S.N.L.*: The Surprising Reason Rosie O'Donnell Didn't Play Steve Bannon," Vanity Fair-HWD, May 15 2017, https://www .vanityfair.com/hollywood/2017/05/snl-rosie-odonnell-steve-bannon -donald-trump-alec-baldwin-sean-spicer-melissa-mccarthy.

make humor happen; you can only let it happen. Humor abhors control. Learning to trust enough to let the humor come through is hard for many and nearly impossible for some because **the root of humor is the embrace of mystery**.

In this way humor is just like righteousness.

In Luke 18:9–14, Jesus tells a parable that gets at the heart of the righteousness trap. I recommend you read it to yourself out loud now. I even put it in the book for you:

> He also told this parable to some who trusted in themselves that they were righteous and regarded others with contempt: "Two men went up to the temple to pray, one a Pharisee and the other a tax collector. The Pharisee, standing by himself, was praying thus, 'God, I thank you that I am not like other people: thieves, rogues, adulterers, or even like this tax collector. I fast twice a week; I give a tenth of all my income.' But the tax collector, standing far off, would not even look up to heaven, but was beating his breast and saying, 'God, be merciful to me, a sinner!' I tell you, this man went down to his home justified rather than the other; for all who exalt themselves will be humbled, but all who humble themselves will be exalted."

Did you notice? The parable is hilarious—if you get it. The Pharisee in the story is a parody of religiosity. He checks all the boxes. He gives the right amount of money. He is so pious that he doesn't just pray; he fasts—and he does that twice a week. He is even a grateful person. He makes a point to thank God. Sure, he is thanking God for not making him like "other" people, but it is still gratitude . . . of a sort. He does everything "right," yet he gets it all wrong.

However, the story praises the tax collector. In the ancient world, the tax collectors made their living by skimming off the top. They were, by definition, corrupt. For Jewish people who were tax collectors, like the one in this parable, it was even worse. He worked for the

Roman oppressors; he was considered a traitor. Yet it was his honesty and his open heart that connected him to God. The Pharisee trusted his own judgment and obedience. The tax collector was desperate enough to trust what God was doing.

Watch out, though. The brilliance of the parable is that as soon as we start judging the Pharisee, the parable flips and we become him. If that seems strange, test yourself. When you were reading the parable, did you think, "I know someone just like that"? If so, you lost the grace, but don't feel bad; it takes time to work up the muscles.

Questions for Deeper Thought

- Have you ever tried to force yourself to pray? What happened?
- Have you ever tried to force your relationship with God?
- Think of some of the most profoundly spiritual moments in your life. What did you have to let go of to meet those moments?
- What are you trying to force in your life right now?

Chapter 2

"Yes," Part 1

The Power of Positivity versus the Whack-A-Mole

E veryone loves positive people, so why are they so rare? I think it is because most of us haven't been taught how to be positive. Even if we give true positivity lip service, few of us are given a safe place to practice what it feels like to face life with radical openness. Consider this your invitation. You don't need to be convinced, but now you can experiment with scandalously simple practice at saying "Yes."

Most people who know anything about improv will tell you that the first rule of improv is to say, "Yes!"[1] That is *kind of* true. It is true enough that it is useless to contradict, plus contradicting it seems to violate the premise anyway. It is also true that in improv we are taught to say, "Yes, &"—and positivity is the doorknob to that

---

1. Quick disclaimer: I mentioned that saying "Yes!" is often talked about as a rule of improv. That itself is an oversimplification. Improv is about freedom, so our general notion of rules doesn't really apply. Rules and freedom are both sides of a flipping coin in improv and spirituality, and we will be playing with this idea throughout the whole book. I said "flipping" coin. Lol. You can decide for yourself if that is a euphemism for swearing.

mansion. "Yes" is about positivity, and even more fundamentally it is the choice to share the reality of another. When we talk about saying "yes" in improv, we are really talking about two different things. The first and most obvious is the power of positivity. The second is the power of the choice to share the other's reality. When these two factors combine, miracles of collaboration start to happen. Interestingly, the sharing reality thing (the nonobvious part of "yes") is where the true teamwork, art, and spiritual wisdom of improv emerges. However, because positivity is the most obvious thing about "yes," we'll start with that.

Power of Positivity

Have you ever noticed how rare it is that people really say "yes"? I mean a real "yes." Not a negotiation, or a qualified "yes," but an enthusiastic "yes." I sometimes joke that this world is so full of "noes" and equivocations that when you put people on stage and they actually say "yes" to each other, it is only funny because we are so tragically starved to see any agreement whatsoever.

Once at a clergy retreat the leader had us do this simple exercise. I was skeptical at first, but I learned a lot from it. He had us stand in two lines with each person facing another. He had one line say, "Yes," and the other line respond, "No." We did that back and forth about twenty times. Then we switched. The "no" group became the "yes" group, and vice versa.

I began to pay attention to how saying "no" so many times in a row felt in my body. I also noticed how it felt when I said "yes." This was before I began improvising, and it was out of character for me to look to my body for wisdom then. But I am glad I did. As it turns out, understanding and listening to your body's wisdom is a huge part of both improv and Christianity, but I had no idea in that moment.

First, I was in the "yes" group. I remember thinking as the exercise started that it was going to suck. I was going to keep saying,

"Yes," and they were going to keep saying "No." I felt like we were going to live my nightmare of late-night church vestry meetings. But an instinct took over. I realized it would be too boring to say "yes" the same way every time, so I started playfully changing how I delivered the one line. I said it as a question, then as a demand. I said it with a little flirty imagery, then with a calm faith that couldn't be shaken by the response. With each word, my sense of power began to grow, but it wasn't *my* power. It felt like it was coming up from the floor, through my body, and out. And to my shock, saying "yes" felt really good. In fact, I wanted more. Saying "yes" became freeing. It allowed me to feel like I was part of something greater, and because I knew there would always be another "yes" coming, I could see right past the "no."

Then came my turn to say, "No." I continued the trick of trying to deliver the lines differently. I began to enjoy that I could shut down my partner's enthusiasm with just a word. It gave me a sense of control that the first exercise did not. It became like a game of whack-a-mole. It was fun, and it made me feel good about me, but that was about it.

What the exercise did was develop biofeedback and muscle memory for collaboration, which is also what improv does. Improvisers need to be able to work together instinctually. We don't have time to think it out. We have to trust each other and go. As it turns out, that skill of being able to collaborate in real time is invaluable for the Christian life too.

Having an active and meaningful connection to God requires active collaboration with the Holy Spirit in the moment. True spiritual gurus or saints are just ordinary people who have cultivated an instinct to trust God. Prayer isn't just reading words on a page or writing a letter to God in your head. Prayer is the experience of belovedness in real time. God can and will speak to just about anyone at any time, but we call prayer a practice for a reason. It is one invaluable part of spiritual training. It is *so* easy to talk yourself out of a trusting relationship with God. It is *so* easy to explain away a spiritual experience. If you want to practice what it feels like to push past those excuses try praying in embarrassing ways. Pray with watercolors. Or, lay down flat with your face to the ground.[2] Make up a ridiculous song that you sing so loud your dog runs away. You could even make God a mixtape.[3] Believe it or not, you have ridiculous and extravagant impulses about how to guide your prayer life. Most Christians have trained themselves to ignore them. We think that if we lock away our ridiculousness it will go away and life will be more manageable. **But ridiculousness is like a puppy. When you lock it inside all day, it will just eat your shoes and pee on your couch.** However, if you start finding ways to be all in with prayer, you will find that life in your soul will become much more enjoyable and rewarding.

Similarly, if you want to have a ministry that truly empowers and lifts the souls of those around you, if you want to unlock your neighbor's heart and hand them the key to the garden of their soul, it starts with full acceptance of the divine image in your neighbor. Train yourself to get curious when someone talks to you about their dreams. If someone has an out-of-the-box idea, give it real consideration and talk to them about what it would look like if it worked. Even if it only ever exists in your shared imagination, that connection itself is more meaningful than the majority of the stuff we do most days. In my church we have an annual holy water squirt gun fight to celebrate our baptism.[4] It is ridiculous. And glorious. If you want to empower your friend's next huge idea, you have to be willing to care for it when it is still small—like a little baby burping in your face. You won't know how to deal with the infinite possibilities of the

---

2. "Prostrate" is the seminary term.

3. "Mixtape" is Gen X for "playlist." Sorry about the antiquated language. I just really wanted it to sound pathetic.

4. I always tell people that they have my guarantee that it will be 100 percent vampire free.

grace around you until you can train yourself to know what the next big "yes" is going to feel like *before* you say it.

When we live in a positive and supportive community, one centered in "yes," it transforms us. I never saw that kind of transformative community in church until I learned how to make it.[5] Even though I lived in churches without this "yes" focus for most of my life, the foundation of the Church is radical acceptance. From the moment when the heavens split at Jesus's baptism and God said, "This is my beloved" to the Last Supper where Jesus said, "I call you friends," the fullness of acceptance and love of God and neighbor has always and will always define the true *ecclesia* (church) of Jesus.

I have no idea why or how we have lost that understanding; most people I know view it as the role of the church to say "no." Jesus is clear that every "Thou shalt not" was written so that we would understand how to love God and our neighbor more fully. It is about loving big, but somehow it got translated, "Be small." Our community's purpose is seen at best as an attempt at behavioral modification and at worse a set of archaic prejudices. Wrap that in power and tie it with the bow of family shame and you turn something beautiful into something ugly. You could look at Christianity and Christian teaching as centuries of rejection and hate. You could make a strong case that the Church is about saying "no." But please don't. The damage we have done proves the power we hold, but there is no divine power in "no." There is just control. The overwhelming power of the Christian faith comes from something beneath the surface. It flows from the consistency of the God who says "yes" to loving us, accepting us, building us up, and living with us.

God created a community to remind us of God's character. I believe God must have known that we would eventually even screw that up, so God gave us scripture to remind us that we come from a bunch of loser disciples so we won't get lost in our mistakes, but

---

5. I will talk about this in section II.

be called back to a supportive, positive relationship with God and each other.

Once we look under the hood and understand that the engine of the church is the power of "yes," then we start to see how the church survived all this time. Why would Jesus send his missionaries out two by two unless being there for each other was a necessity for mission and ministry? Why would Jesus have been heartbroken and angry in the garden that all his friends had fallen asleep on the eve of his execution, unless their actual support of each other mattered?

Then we can pivot back and reunderstand Christian history. Even the people we celebrate most are often misunderstood. For most of my life I assumed that the saints of the church lived in isolation. The more that I have talked to parishioners about this, the more I have realized I was not alone in my thinking. The saints are imagined as always calm. They are giving, but distant and independent. Somehow, we imagine these sacred gurus reached spiritual fulfillment on their own and their works of wisdom and charity were tossed out to the church like bread crumbs on a duck pond. But that isn't the case. Athanasius was . . . well, I wouldn't describe him as nice. The Cappadocians (the people who came up with the Trinity) were bitingly sarcastic, and there is even a legend that Jolly Old St. Nicholas punched a heretic in the face at the Council of Nicaea.

Even more fundamental is the way that saints make other saints. If you look at Christian history, saints tend to show up in bunches. Francis and Claire, for example, or Teresa of Avila and John of the Cross. In many cases we even have exchanges of letters between saints and their soul-friends to show us the extravagant care, support, and affection they showed each other.[6]

What's my point? I have two. One, sainthood is much more like the daily life we live than it is like still waters or a lavender bath. And

6. Vincent J. O'Malley, *Saintly Companions: A Cross-Reference of Sainted Relationships* (New York: Alba House, 1995).

two, Christianity is a team sport. Sainthood is something we learn from each other in a blessed committee, not a detached individual transcendence.[7]

Sticky Faith

We have seen the power of "yes" in the Bible and in Christian history; now let's take it to a more personal level. I have been a priest now for over a dozen years, and every chance I get I ask people to talk about how they found faith or why they are at church. Not once in those years has someone told me that the reason they are there is because one day they started reading the Bible out of curiosity. Every single time I have been told about someone who was influential in their life who believed in them. The Sunday school teacher who slipped circular butter cookies on their little fingers. The acolyte master who was rough but made sure they knew which order to light the candles. The youth program volunteer who was a second mama and they all knew it. In my case, it was a man named James who used to take my mom aside and tell her, "God has a hand on that child." James died of AIDS when I was in the fourth grade and I have taken the cross he left me everywhere I have ever traveled. Sometimes the story of finding faith also includes a profound experience in church worship or at a youth camp, but I have never heard of the seed of spiritual experience taking root unless there was someone outside of the individual who chose to water it. Someone who saw what was underneath the soil and believed not just in God but in the person who was coming to him.

As it turns out, we have data to back this up. In the nineties, churches poured money and resources into youth ministry. Not just

---

7. If you are looking for detached individual transcendence, there are religions out there I can recommend. Or recommend-ish. Sorry, I am in love with the idea of truly supportive community. And yes, I do realize that truly supportive community means giving the introverts the distance they need.

youth groups and Sunday school classes, but separate youth services started popping up all over the place. With the expanse of the evangelical Christian movement, there was a push to make church for the cool kids. Not to go off too far on a tangent, but that is hilarious to me. Read the Bible. Christianity has always been for losers and misfits. Yet just like the colonizing missionaries of the Middle Ages trying to convert the kings by first offering them Jesus with a side of gunpowder, we went after the ruling cliques armed with candy, bounce houses, and huge flat screens. A group called Sticky Faith has done exhaustive study of this time and what they found was that if we were looking at creating lifelong relationships with Jesus and something that resembles what we believed was Christian faith, for the most part we failed hard. Their research shows that most of these youth ministries didn't nurture a faith that could survive the crucible of adolescence, much less the challenge of defining yourself in young adulthood.[8]

After this study came out, youth workers and pastors started pairing it with their experiences and a new realization is beginning to emerge. We have been doing everything backwards. We thought, "Get the kids, then their friends, and so on." We told parents to send us their kids, and we will teach them faith. Then we focused on the peer relationships of the youth to try to make sure we had "critical mass" for them to enjoy themselves and want to come back. But as it turns out, most of the youth who genuinely knew and understood the Christian story didn't learn it at church; they learned it at home. And most youth ministry professionals believe that the biggest predictor of a true meaningful lifelong Christian faith is not whether they have peers to go to church with, it is whether the youth have five significant relationships with adults of faith in addition to their parents. Put more simply: a would-be Christian needs people in

---

8. "Sticky Faith," The Fuller Youth Institute, accessed October 29, 2021, https://fulleryouthinstitute.org/stickyfaith.

their life with the authority to say, "Yes, this is God, and he is working on you."

The Bible tells us that as a church we are all members of one body,[9] which means that we cannot survive without each other. From a great distance Paul was imploring his church plant to stop bickering with each other and to live in the kind of harmony, love, and affirmation that defined the gospel as he preached it. The fact that he had to write that letter is itself proof that living in community is hard. Making community means giving up our assumptions about what our neighbor is going to do and being honest when it hurts. Acceptance of the other is the road to connection and transformation. But most of us don't know how to make community the way Paul did. He was one of those rare people who knew how to say a real "yes," and it made him the greatest evangelist in history. Saying a real "yes" is rare for one simple reason. Unlike Paul, most of us don't have a lot of practice.

Improv teaches us to have the instinct to say "yes." I think that instinct is one the church needs to relearn and reclaim if we want to be able to find joy in our identity, theology, and our communal dance with the divine.

If you don't believe me, read *Interior Castle* by Teresa of Avila or any of the great works of mystical theology. They all say the same thing. The path to true deep and powerful communion with God is not easy, but it is available to all God's children. **We are all beloved of God, which means anyone can be brilliant and beautiful. But no one can be brilliant or beautiful without someone to tell them that they are.** That is why the ability to say a real "yes" can change a person or even a community forever.

---

9. 1 Corinthians 12:12ff.

Delivery and Why Jesus Is the Ultimate "Yes" Man

One of the things we learn in improv is that delivery can change everything. There is a game called "pick a play" where three improvisers have a scene. The first player can say whatever they want, but the other two are given different plays or comic books and all of the lines those players can say have to come from those books. That is right: take an improv class and you might find yourself trying to make a scene where everything one of your partners says comes out of *A Streetcar Named Desire*, and the other's lines are drawn from *The Butter Battle Book* by Dr. Seuss. It is funny every time to see people struggle, but experienced improvisers will make it work, and I promise you it is like witnessing a miracle.

Imagine three performers enter the stage. The first player starts miming like he is a bartender. He looks up at the other two and starts the scene:

> **Bartender:** Frank! Susie! Good to see you again. What will you have today?
> **Frank:** *(madly flipping through the Dr. Suess book)* Sour, Cherry Stone Pits.
> **Bartender:** Of course, our specialty. How about you, Susie? You want something to drink today?
> **Susie:** *(looks down at her copy of* Streetcar, *then up again at the bartender, then yells at the top of her lungs)* Stella!!!!!!!!!!
> **Bartender:** Oh yeah, we have that on tap.

My point is that text can be read thousands of different ways. Changing the tone or context can drastically change the meaning. Realizing this changed the way I approach the Bible. The seminary I went to was really into having worship services. I remember once talking to a Methodist student from the seminary across the street. She was complaining about how often they have chapel services there. She explained that they have a service every day and that all students are required to go to at least one service a week. I laughed. When she asked why, I explained that my seminary had three services per day, and students were required to go to at least one. I could say a lot about the value of regular worship as a practice, but my point is that at every one of those services we read one to three (often lengthy) passages of scripture out loud. Going to chapel daily, I noticed the students would often slip into harsh or even judgmental tones as they read words of scripture. This was common with passages from the Hebrew Bible, but it applied to the words of Jesus too. I knew intellectually that the other students didn't really think God was like that, but the temptation for any of us to hear judgment or attack is incredibly strong. It pulls us in like the gravity of a black hole. I began to be aware that if we delivered the exact same lines differently, the whole passage could feel different and way more consistent with the God I knew.

Let's take one of the harshest-speaking and just generally strangest prophets in the Bible: John the Baptist. John ditched the comfort of the city and set up camp on the river Jordan, which was the boundary between the Promised Land and the desert. His location was not just one of convenience; it was intentional. It was the same desert that the ancient Israelites wandered in for forty years to escape slavery. John proclaimed the coming of the Messiah and the day of reckoning. He called people to repent, which literally means to turn around from sin and back toward God.

John was a purist and pretty intense. To remind him of his sins, he wore camel hair because it was scratchy. He subsisted on locusts and wild honey. He spent his days preaching and baptizing people. The word "baptism" in Greek is just the ordinary word for "wash," so he was washing people in the river to symbolize how they were letting their sins go. John must have made for quite a show because he got a lot of attention. Eventually, some religious elites called Pharisees and Sadducees started coming. Maybe they came to see what the fuss was all about; maybe to see how they could cash in on John's popularity. John didn't like it one bit, and when those elites started getting in line for baptism, he told them he thought they were a bunch of phonies: "You brood of vipers! Who warned you to flee from the wrath to come?" (Matt. 3:7b).

Now when we read that in church, usually from a raised pulpit or from a golden book, it feels kind of fun to read it harshly. Maybe some of it is that I am generally so careful as a preacher that there is part of me that would love to open a sermon with "You den of snakes!" I don't actually feel that way about my congregants, but I think every preacher dreams of being at least 30 percent more badass. John was 100 percent badass. This is why it is important to understand your body's reactions. It feels fun to read with judgment. It feels like whack-a-mole. It feels like saying "no" on repeat.

As an experiment, imagine with me that there might be another way of delivering the same line. One that maybe has more of the grace and forgiveness embedded in it, the kind we see in the overarching story of Christianity. What if instead of screaming, "You brood of vipers!" John said it softer while shaking his head? What if he delivered it more like a loving father who caught his kid with his hand in the cookie jar?[10] Then, instead of imagining John pointing his finger and saying, "Who warned you to flee from the wrath that is to come?" as if he thought those people shouldn't flee because they deserved the wrath, what if he said it sarcastically? They were supposed to be religious elites and experts. The Sadducees ran the temple for God's sake. What were they doing out on the fringes? What if John was trying

---

10. English majors may want to point out that there is an exclamation point at the end of the "brood of vipers" line. Fun fact: the New Testament was written before punctuation was invented. So there was no exclamation mark or period in the original text. The punctuation is there just because of the way the translators assumed the passage should be read.

to shake them out of playacting at repentance? What if his tone was more like, "Who warned *you* of the 'wrath' that is to come?"

John went on to tell them that they couldn't trust in their heritage or position. If they wanted to get in on what God is doing, they would have to get real. We automatically assume that we should read the text as a condemnation, but it just as easily could be read as an intervention, and even as an invitation to be part of the Messiah Jesus who would grind away their fake protective exterior (chaff) and expose what is truly spiritually nourishing (the wheat).

I don't know why human beings seem to enjoy the judgment game so much. Worse yet, we like to play it when we are both judge and defendant. While whack-a-mole is fun, Jesus is clear that judgment is not a game for us,[11] and other parts of the Bible go so far as to say that we are stealing God's turf if we play it.[12]

The next time you are trying to decide how to deliver one of Jesus's lines, remember that in his day what was seen as special, scandalous, and dangerous about Jesus wasn't his condemnation, but his acceptance. They didn't kill him because he said "no." They killed him because he said "yes" way too much.

Jesus as "Yes" Man

It is right there in John's gospel: "For God so loved the world that he gave his only Son, so that everyone who believes in him may not perish but may have eternal life. Indeed, God did not send the Son into the world to condemn the world, but in order that the world might be saved through him."[13] If the summary isn't enough, let's get into the specifics.

---

11. Mathew 7:1–3
12. James 4:12
13. John 3:16–17

In Luke 15, Jesus tells a series of parables all set to undermine the game of whack-a-mole that was expected from the religious leaders. They didn't like the people that Jesus was spending time with, so Jesus told parables to try to underscore the value of those they sought to exclude. The second of these stories is the prodigal son. It is a beautiful story, and it is interesting to me how often it is truncated. I have found that when you ask someone who has been going to church their whole life to tell the story, they tell it like this:

> There was a son who was ungrateful and wanted to ditch his dad and move out on his own. He asked for his inheritance even though his father was still alive. The son went out and wasted his money and ended up poor and hungry. He realized that his father's workers were treated better than he was, so he rehearsed a lengthy apology as he walked to see his dad. When his dad saw him from far off, he ran to him, hugged him, and forgave him before he had a chance to apologize. They put a fancy robe on the son, gave him some bling, and had a huge party. The point is, no matter how bad it has gotten, no matter the wrong you have done, God will forgive you.

All those points are in the story, but they aren't the point of the story. Keen student of the Bible that I am sure you are, you probably noticed I dropped the sibling as I told the story above. Jesus doesn't just talk about one son; he talks about two. The son who went away was the youngest. When he returned, the father accepted him while the older son threw a fit and huffed out of the party. Then the desperate father went to the older son to tell him that he loved him, and pled with him to understand why they should celebrate that the younger was back.

In context, the parable is aimed at the religious elite. They were the older son who was missing out because they saw the merciful way of the father as unfair. The Bible often trades on sibling relationships, but I think the point is more profound here. God is merciful, and mercy is unfair—even scandalous. The father was in trouble with the older son for the same reason Jesus was in trouble with the Pharisees: because he was too accepting and affirming. He was saying "yes" and it was ruining their game of whack-a-mole.

Similarly, in the parable of the vineyard,[14] Jesus tells a story about a landowner who hired workers at different times during the day so some worked more hours than others. At the end of the day the landowner paid everyone for a full day's work, even those who had started in the evening. The workers who served the whole day got angry. They claimed they should have gotten more, even though they were given everything they were promised. After a bit of a back-and-forth, the landowner gave this scathing retort: "Are you envious that I am generous?"

Jesus was constantly in political trouble because he crossed racial, cultural, social, economic, and religious lines to include those that were rejected. And almost all his famous parables are designed to shake the listener to a place where they are willing to accept, to say "yes" to those they would have otherwise rejected.

Despite what our conventional American wisdom might suggest, **Jesus wasn't murdered for what he rejected. Jesus was murdered for who he accepted. He was brutally tortured and killed in the most painful and humiliating way imaginable because he hung out with the wrong people.**

Exercise "Yes" and "No"

Learning the instinct of saying "yes" takes practice. If you can't (or don't have the courage to) find a partner to do the "yes"/"no" exercise I described in this chapter, find time at home with a mirror. Put on some music that inspires you or loosens you up and try it. Try saying

---

14. Matthew 20:1–16

"yes" a dozen different ways and notice how that feels in your body. Then try saying "no" a dozen different ways. Journal about the experience. Draw an outline of a person and note what parts of your body were responding in each case. If you want to harness the power of positivity, it cannot just come from your mind—you need to teach yourself how you feel it.　•

Chapter 3

"Yes," Part 2
The Dramatic Conclusion

The Power of Sharing Reality

Wow! So much "yes." And if you recall, we haven't even gotten to the good part yet. Improv teachers encourage positivity a lot, but that is not technically what the "yes" is. It is delightfully scandalous to see positivity on stage, but improvisers are not taught to ignore the literal word "no": they are taught to avoid what is called a "denial." You are not expected or required to respond positively to your partner. What you are expected to do is agree to work together to share the same reality.

This is an important technical difference, so let me give some examples. If one player comes out, mimes like he is holding a gun, and says, "I am going to shoot you!" you say, "No!" While that is a negative statement, you have agreed that it is in fact a gun, and you have added the idea that you value your life. That is a negatively phrased "yes" because it accepts the *reality* your partner is offering.

On the other hand, if your partner comes out, mimes like he is holding a gun, and says, "I am going to shoot you!" and you say, "That is not a gun; it is a fish," you can't have much of a scene because you are arguing over the nature of the reality you share. That is a denial. There are literally millions of ways to respond that are a "yes." If you say, "Go ahead and shoot me, I am Superman," while you puff out your chest, you have offered something to work with. Sometimes even if a player literally says "no," it can cement the shared reality.

Here is a real-life improv example. Once I was in a scene set in a dentist office. I was the patient. The dentist came up to me with pliers in her hand, and in a thick German accent told me to sit still because she was going to pull all my teeth without anesthetic. My instinct was to say, "No. Stop. My precious teeth," but I buried that and said, "Umm . . . okay. Yes. Go ahead." Now that could have been funny and led to an interesting scene about a person who didn't care about their teeth, but that wasn't what I was doing. Our teacher called time and explained that if I had said, "No, please don't," that would have been agreement from an improv perspective. It would have been saying "yes" to the reality we were living in. If I had said, "You're no dentist; you're a tax attorney. That is why I've been carrying this briefcase for you," that would have been a denial. The difficulty doesn't arise from a disagreement between the characters. It arises from a disagreement between the actors if they are fighting each other about the nature of the imagined reality in the scene.

Here is another example from one of the oldest, most respected books on improv comedy.

> Denials are taboo in improvisation. Being a good player means having ethics. One of the best examples of denial occurred during the early days of Second City, when Del [Close] and Joan Rivers were in the same company, and it rankles him to this day.
>
> One night in an improvised scene Joan told Del that she wanted a divorce. Del responded as an emotionally distraught husband might, in the hope of getting her to reconsider. "But

honey, what about the children?" She replied, "We don't have any children!"

Naturally she got a huge laugh. Naturally she had completely destroyed the scene.[1]

I would like to add that even if someone gives you a denial, that doesn't mean that you should give up. I can't help but wonder what would have happened in that last example if once the laugh had cleared, Del had said, "I don't know how many times I have to tell you, just because they are adopted doesn't mean they are not our children." Bam. That would have created a scene about a callous, unfeeling mother and a dad who was trying desperately to make her care. Denial is bad, but you can still make your way out of it.

Choosing to share in someone's reality has always been a vital part of our spiritual tradition, and it is hard to imagine a time in our history when it has been more important than the information age. More and more it seems like people are living in separate realities with separate groups of facts and less and less empathy for those outside their bubble.

The church has been guilty of this for a long time. When we moved from the outskirts of society in the very beginning to being a central institution in the Roman Empire and beyond, we also became the arbiter of right and wrong, of fact and fiction. People often make a case for how Galileo was mistreated and condemned by the church, but at the time the church was the only arbiter of knowledge. Yes, he was right, but his theories were far from finished. I am not defending what the church did; I am saying that the problem was deeper, that the church became the bubble. It became the clique deciding who was in and who was out. It started playing whack-a-mole and lost its vocation of being in the world though not of it.

---

1. Charna Halpern and Del Close, *Truth in Comedy: The Manual of Improvisation* (Colorado Springs, CO: Meriwether Publishing, 1994), 48.

"Yes" Is Validation

Anyone who has ever gotten into a fight with a loved one and has made up knows one thing: validation is the beginning of healing relationships. When I work with couples in premarital counseling, I start with a ridiculously simple exercise that I got from a group called Prepare/Enrich.[2] It is called the "I Wish" exercise.

It is a communication exercise. The couples go back and forth: one the speaker, the other the listener. The speaker says, "I wish," and then something they want more of (or less of) in the relationship; then they state how they would feel if that came true. I explain that this exercise is not about whether to do the thing they are talking about. It is not a negotiation; it is just about having one person share how they feel and the other person showing that they understand. One of the things couples counselors find is that a ridiculous number of fights happen because couples jump to trying to resolve the issue without understanding what the problem is first.

So the speaker says something like, "I wish we would have more intimate time, and if we did I wouldn't feel so lonely every day," or, "I wish we wouldn't spend so much time just sitting on the couch, because I don't want to feel like I am wasting my life," or, "I wish you wouldn't tell your mom everything about our life, because then I would feel less judged."

The other partner summarizes what they heard and then they are supposed to ask, "Did I get that right?" It is often extremely awkward to teach this exercise at first. People will say what they wish, but neglect to say how it would make them feel—that is because sharing your feelings is the most vulnerable part. I can usually get the receiver to understand that they are just trying to summarize the issue and not resolve it, but teaching people to actually check in and ask, "Did I get that right?" is tough because that is also vulnerable.

---

2. Prepare/Enrich, https://www.prepare-enrich.com/

It might expose the fact that they missed something important. It takes practice to teach the receiver that the reason to check is to make sure that they have gotten what the partner needed to say. In this way the receiver is encouraging the sharer to give, and the sharer is helping the receiver understand.

Most of the couple work I do is premarital counseling, so often the couples come in positive and happy and even dreamy about each other, but this exercise is like magic. It gets to deep issues quickly. It is interesting that after a full session of doing this exercise, the couple almost always leaves seeming much more deeply bonded. We literally haven't fixed anything. Well, except one thing: that which was unheard became heard. Each partner was given directions and permission to step into the other's reality in a way that is appreciative and attentive. From an improv perspective, that is a "yes," and it is remarkable how healing just a simple "yes" can be.

Of course, teaching someone else to say "yes" is one thing; having the courage to do it is another. Let me give you a practical example of what sharing a person's reality can do in an everyday ministry setting.

That God Is Awful

Once after an improv class a group of us went to hang out and debrief. In the beginning especially, those times are valuable. Everyone is vulnerable, everyone feels awkward, so everyone is ridiculously complementary. "You felt stupid? No! You were hilarious! I was embarrassing. . . . Really, you liked the thing with the hat?" All night long. Just unwavering support and positivity. It is fantastic. The backbiting doesn't start happening until you start performing, but that's another story.

After a while most of the group had dispersed and I was talking with one of my classmates. I suspected that she wanted to talk to me because I am a pastor. It is strange when you have been doing this priestly work for a while. You begin to see tells that other people don't see. Maybe that isn't professional; maybe it is just a byproduct of caring. You see things like a subtle nervousness or a difficulty asking for something that has already been offered, or a hyper-intensive drive to competency, all of which point to something: a history of abuse. In *Star Wars Episode III: The Revenge of the Sith*, Obi-Wan Kenobi is looking for a planet that he believes all record of was deleted from the archives. He goes to Yoda to find out what to do. Yoda tells him if the planet isn't on the map, look for how the other planets have been moved by the gravity of the "deleted" planet. Spotting the spiritual and emotional wounds in a person is like that. They will usually reveal the shadow of the gravity of the thing long before they will point you to it.

Sure enough, this woman had lived through hell growing up. She had one of the hardest, ugliest stories of abuse I have ever heard, and I have heard some painful stuff. I was grateful for her courage in telling me, and I was glad that it wasn't my first time hearing a story like that. The good news was she was dealing with her stuff. She didn't think of herself this way, but it was obvious that her resilience was legitimately amazing. She was taking improv classes because she knew that she needed to find more confidence talking to big corporate types. I listened, empathized the best I could, and made sure that she knew that I respected all the choices she had made to move forward in her life. I did all the intake things clergy do, making sure that she had a path to therapy and more support. We talked about what the cycle of abuse did and how she had been in survival mode all her life and how I was impressed that she was learning how to thrive.

Then we got to the thing that she really wanted to talk to me about: God. Talking about God is always tricky. I am glad that the Holy Spirit was there to do the real work of the conversation. It is tricky because, for good or ill, our experience of people colors the way we experience God. I talked to an orphan once who said that he could never believe in God because he didn't have parents. Similarly, those who have known pure unconditional love and acceptance are much more likely to be able to wrap their brains around the truth that God is calling out to our souls 24-7.

When someone has had a significant experience of abuse, especially in childhood, especially in their family, there are layers upon layers of shame and self-doubt. It is a psychological minefield. There are triggers underfoot, but all the ground looks the same.

We will call this woman Stephanie. She explained that her abusive family took her to church—not a lot, but often enough. Her father was treated with great honor there despite what she knew of him from home. She talked about going to church and getting beaten as soon as they got home. She talked about how everyone at the church was nice to people's faces but then gossiped about them as soon as their backs were turned. She said the sermons were always centered on how sinful the world outside was and how you had to be careful or you would be sent to hell.

Then she said, "That has always been what God has been like for me. Someone who is just waiting for me to step out of line for a second so he could smack me down." She paused and continued, "But I don't know. Is it okay that I don't go to church?"

"Darn it," I thought to myself. First off, it was ridiculous that I got to weigh in on what this precious and battered soul did, as if I were the judge of what was right or wrong; second, I had been in this situation before and I had never felt like what I normally said next did anything to help anyone but myself. I was supposed to say, "God isn't like that at all. God isn't an abusive parent. Don't put on God what belongs on your family. I believe that God loves you and is proud of you and nurtures you even now." I believed all those things, and I had said them before, but it seemed pointless. If someone says, "God hates me," and another replies, "No, God loves you," the conversation stops and both go away feeling hated and alone because all they are doing is arguing over reality.

Then I thought about what we had learned that night in class about how the beginning of working together in improv is deciding to share the other person's reality; once you do that, you can go anywhere together. So I said something that I normally would not have thought of.

"That God sounds like an asshole—and I wouldn't want to worship him either."

All of a sudden, the thought trap snapped like the big wafer at the Eucharist. She laughed, then I chuckled. We started talking more about how the way we understood God mattered, and how people often use Christianity to do harm and how we hated that. In the end, she became one of the most valuable members of my congregation. She changed careers. She stopped working with executives and started working with children. Through the power of the play she learned in improv, she recovered her childhood as an adult. Later she told me that she thought if she hadn't had that conversation that night, she would have ended up dead. This amazing, brilliant, capable, hardworking woman would have been lost to this world, and all it took to switch the track was one person who was willing to join her in her thinking rather than try to correct it.

Nonanxious Presence Is a Nonhelpful Construct

Seminary trained me well on what *not* to say to people like Stephanie. You have probably heard the advice too. There is a whole list. Don't say "God has a plan" or "God doesn't give you more than you can handle." "Go and sin no more" is also contraindicated. You don't want to say anything that implies they had it coming, or that they were asking for it, or that it is a punishment for what they have done. Basically, the rule is don't say anything that will make *you* feel better about hearing the situation. You don't want to bail on their experience. If you do, it will feel like God has bailed on them too. Don't get me wrong, you set boundaries and limits, you need to know when to call it a night, but there is a reason they believe that they are worthless, unworthy of love, and that no one cares about them. It is because that has literally been beaten into them.

The problem is while we are good at teaching would-be pastors and sympathetic laypeople what not to say, we are not always as good at telling them what to say. One of the most repeated phrases in seminary in regards to pastoral care is to be a "nonanxious presence." I never understood why my colleagues loved saying that so much. It is still a negative formulation. There are a lot of ways to be nonanxious. I could be apathetic and be nonanxious. A brick wall in a clerical collar is nonanxious. I always wanted to write a scene where someone is talking to a pastor about God while the pastor is asleep and the pastor gets an A in pastoral care.

Of course, part of the reason for the ambiguity is that any mantra is cookie-cutter. It is one size fits all. The way *you* give Christian care needs to be grounded in who *you* are. Your mantra for pastoral care should be tailored to your personality. What positive would you substitute for nonanxious? Is it calm, or peaceful, or nurturing? Is it patient or gentle? Personally, I am a ball of energy. No joke. Ask any of my congregants. I am the priestly equivalent of a chihuahua. I work to replace nonanxious with an engaged presence.

Exercise in Pastoral Character Building

The question, "What do you replace 'nonanxious' with?" isn't rhetorical. I want you to answer it. When someone brings you heavy stuff or even joyful stuff, how do you want your presence to be felt? Replace nonanxious for yourself with a positively worded adjective. Here are a few for you to consider from the Bible:

- Patient
- Kind
- Appreciative
- Humble
- Honoring
- Self-giving

- Calm
- Forgiving
- Joyfully honest
- Protecting
- Trusting
- Hopeful
- Persevering or steadfast

- _____

You may have guessed that I adapted that list from the hymn to love (1 Cor. 13:4–7). These are all attributes of God-like love, so perhaps you could say a "loving" presence? But I don't recommend you start with "loving presence" because it is too general and too easy to lose your individual way of expressing God's love. Instead, I suggest that you circle one or two or write in another and try it on for a while. Write it on a post-it and put it where you will see it once a day. Take it as a suggestion for how to deal with the plethora of needs we are assaulted with every day. If you find that one isn't making it easier for you to know what to do in those ministry moments, try another one for a month. •

The Logic of the Incarnation and the Pedagogy of Salvation *(Don't worry, I find this subtitle pretentious too.)*

The more I thought about this life-changing encounter with Stephanie and so many others I had in ministry, the more I began to believe that this is how God works. Then it hit me: the Incarnation, stupid. Healing through joining in the reality of the other is the Christian story. God so loved the world that God sent Jesus. God came in person to share our mortal life with all of its pains and heartbreak, and, in Jesus's case, torture and death. Christmas is the season where we celebrate God leaving the bubble of heaven, dropping the whack-a-mole mallet of condemnation, and joining us in our reality long enough to change it.

Sam Wells's Analogy

Anglican priest Sam Wells wrote a fantastic book on improvisation, Christian ethics, and theology called *Improvisation: The Drama
of Christian Ethics*.[3] In many ways, it is the theoretical foundation for
this book, which is intended to be a practical guide to the implementation of his approach. I once heard Wells speak about his book. What
I call "Yes, &" he called "overacceptance." To illustrate that concept,
he used an old story. It is my understanding that it is based on a true
story. Here is my best recollection of it:

> Once there was a fancy concert for a classical piano player.
> The musician was renowned and had traveled far to this large
> auditorium filled with people in evening gowns and tuxedos
> with tails. Just as the pianist began to sit to play, a little girl
> ran up from the audience onto the stage and plopped down on
> the bench next to the performer. Then she began to bang out
> "Chopsticks" with her pointer fingers on the keys. The room
> was tense. Would the pianist walk out in disgust? Would he
> push the child off the bench and just proceed as planned?
> Neither. The pianist reached around the child to improvise
> harmonies to go along with the melody that the child was
> plunking out. After Wells finished the story, he told us that as
> he sees it, that is how God acts over and over again in the Bible.

The choice to sit down and reach around and make music
together—that is the God I know and have been searching for all my
life. When I heard that story for the first time, I felt like I finally understood all the talk, debate, and study we had about grace in seminary.
And it is hilarious to think, right? All those religious people leading their whole lives afraid of retribution. How did we take the most
loving and marvelous being there has ever been, how did we take

---

3. Samuel Wells, *Improvisation: The Drama of Christian Ethics* (Grand Rapids,
MI: Brazos Press, 2004).

the life sacrifice and resurrection of Jesus, and turn it into a story of "Watch out, or the sadistic jerk God will smack you down"? Don't get me wrong, it is sad that we did that, but you have to laugh as well. It's natural to laugh when the thought trap snaps like a host. **The choice to share the reality of those who are suffering is the logic behind the Incarnation itself. "Meeting people where they are" isn't just a good strategy. It is salvation's root.**

The Dramatic Conclusion

If you want to share in the drama of a human life with its ups and downs and *actually make a difference*, you will be doomed to fail if you are stuck arguing over the nature of reality. So this is the conclusion that comes from deeply understanding both the incarnation of Jesus and the "yes" of improv: share reality, and join people in their drama because that is what heals.

The church can be the arbiter of truth, or it can be the instrument of healing, but it cannot be both. The church's historical role of privilege tempts us to become the moral judge of society. I am not sure that position is even open in the world of the information age, but you can tell we miss it. The church misses being important just because it exists. But this antiquated role isn't what Jesus ever had in mind for his followers. The historical privilege of the church tempts us to step over the muck of people in their real lives so that we can sit on a throne and commentate from a safe distance. But that is not what Jesus did. He stepped into the world as it was, and in doing so revealed what it could be.

I understand why accepting someone else's version of reality can seem intimidating. Often, we are afraid to give that much power away. We are concerned by getting trapped in heresy or mistake, but our judgment will not protect us, nor our neighbor. As it turns out, just because you accept a reality as a given, it doesn't mean you are stuck there. That is what the "&" is for in "Yes, &."

Chapter 4

The Comma in "Yes, &"

In all my studies of the nature and virtue of the "Yes, &" approach, I have never heard anyone talk about the comma between the "yes" and the "&," or at least not directly. "Yes" means sharing your partner's reality unconditionally. The "&" is a fierce commitment to make bold choices in the moment to support and work with your partner. There is, however, a place in between that. There is a place where we find the faith and the courage it takes to step into the "&." Hopefully as you grow as an improviser (and Christian) that comma gets shorter and shorter, but to me it represents the trust and even faith it takes to proceed in cocreating something new when you don't know how it will turn out. When I was initially taught improv, this was given to me as a rule: "Trust your partner, trust yourself." **In my experience there are two kinds of people: those who know how to trust others, and those who know how to trust themselves. Someone who knows how to do both is unstoppable.**

How often do we talk about trust? Biblically speaking, faith isn't a matter of intellectual certainty; it is a decision to be in all the way. That means that trust is what makes faith feasible. I'm not saying it's easy; I have been plagued with self-doubt since before I can remember. I was definitely one of those people who knew how to trust others. It feels much less comfortable to trust myself. But one way or another, I have yet to meet the person who is free of any trust issues.

But I'd like to point out something. For all our skepticism, nothing in our world—even our completely secular, big-box business world—works without trust. No one goes to a job unless they trust a paycheck is coming. No war ends until both sides choose to trust that on some rudimentary level, the other party will respect the agreement. The first of the Ten Commandments about "not taking the Lord's name in vain" was not a prohibition of swearing, nor a command to respect. It was the ancient form of contract law. When you would make an agreement with another person, because the ancient world didn't really have courts or signatures, you would say, "May Yahweh [the proper name of God][1] strike me down if I don't comply with this agreement." If you didn't keep your end of the contract, you used the Lord's name in vain. This is to say that trust in human relationships is so indispensable that we have leveraged God to keep humans working together for at least as long as we have history.

Trust and Economics

The ubiquitous necessity for trust goes even deeper than enforcing agreements. It goes to the basis of our entire economic and monetary system. In 1929, the stock market crash was bad. Worse than the crash was that people got the idea that they could no longer trust the banks to give them back their money. I was an economics major, so I would love to go on and on about the specifics of this process, but basically banks create more money in the system by taking and lending money, which means when banks fail, actual money evaporates. The

---

1. So much reverence has been ascribed to the name "Yahweh" because of the commandment not to take God's name in vain that even in the Bible "Yahweh" is translated by putting a different word in all capital letters: "LORD." That means "Yaweh." If it says "Lord," that is actually the word for "Lord."

run on the banks decreased the overall supply of money. From 1930 to 1933, the money supply in the US fell by 30 percent.[2] Why? It wasn't because the banks weren't doing their job. It was because trust was lost. For that matter, why did the stock market crash in the first place? Not because the business that those stocks represented all of a sudden became less profitable. On October 23, 1929, people believed that the stocks had real value, so they did. On October 24, that changed. Then with the run on the banks, the same thing happened again. When trust disappears, people will run like lemmings off a cliff: the Great Depression is proof. Later, as a call to recovery, FDR famously said, "The only thing you have to fear is fear itself." That isn't just amazing rhetoric. It is LITERALLY true. It was a crisis of trust that nearly obliterated the entire global economic system. Sometimes people wonder why on the dollar bill it says, "In God we trust." While the history of that move is complicated, I like to point out that the government has every incentive to make sure that you have faith in its currency just to keep our economy functioning. It is "the LORD's name in vain," take two.

Trust and Medicine

One more illustration of the importance of trust: what we believe actually affects our bodies. Now stay with me. I know that a lot of my readers are thinking, "Uh oh, he is about to get New Agey." I am not. I am going to get sciencey. You probably understand whenever the FDA approves a study of a drug it needs to be a double-blind study. In a double-blind study, the patient doesn't know if she is getting the real drug or a fake, and the health care worker administering that medication doesn't know if it is real or a fake. Think for a second of

---

2. Gary Richardson, "The Great Depression," *Federal Reserve History*, November 22, 2013, https://www.federalreservehistory.org/essays/great -depression.

the sheer number of studies that happen in a given year, and the millions of dollars we spend on medical studies. Now think about how much more staff and logistics are required to deliver medication that we *know* is physically useless. Why do we do that? Because we have proof that if patients trust that they are getting medication that will help them, it will help at least some of them. This is called the placebo effect. The patient's simple belief that they are being treated can make pain or illness improve or disappear, even without other cures. This is not some hippie-dippy rant on the healing power of drum circles; this is proven medical science. Most of us have just never stopped to think about the logical consequences of it.[3]

Trust *matters.* It is the stitchwork holding not just our lives, but our society together. Yet for all of the difference trust makes, most of us are barely aware of how to grow it. Some doubt you even can grow trust, but people do constantly. It is just usually grown in small increments over time.

Building Trust and Finding Faith

Sometimes trust comes as a gift, but most of the time it needs to be earned with patience and practice. Researcher Brené Brown has done a lot of work on studying how people form trust. She has noted that trust is usually formed in the little things—remembering a grandmother's name, going out of your way to give a vote of encouragement. Trust is lost in similar small and simple ways. She calls this process of making trust between friends "marble jar friends," after

---

3. By the way, if you ever want to drive a theologically conservative Christian crazy, just say, "You know Jesus didn't heal those people . . . and neither did God." When they are like, "Yes, Jesus most certainly did," say, "Well, you can believe what you want, but unlike you I believe what Jesus says." When they seem perplexed at that, just say, "Yeah. Jesus said, 'Your faith has made you well.'" He didn't say, "I healed you," or "God healed you." Jesus is saying it is the placebo effect. Maybe I shouldn't have said that. That thought might fester.

a jar that her daughter's teacher kept on her desk. The teacher would put a marble in the jar every time the class behaved well, and would take one out whenever they lost a piece of her trust.[4] I can't tell you what I would give for a real-time visual representation of the trust of those around me. Sadly we don't walk around with marble jars of the current trust level balanced on our head. For this reason, trust is something we have to practice, and improv gives us the tools both to think about that and to actually do it. This returns me to a rule I was taught: "Trust your partner, trust yourself." Of course, it is one thing to order trust; it is another to cultivate it over time—that takes practice.

Most people visibly cringe when you suggest a trust game. As a kid I never went to camp, so I don't understand the bizarre collective trauma surrounding that experience, but if nothing else trust games make it super easy to diagnose your relationship to trust. If trust games are a living hell for you, then you probably already know how to trust yourself, but not so much others. Conversely, when it comes to trust fall time and they tell you, "Stiff as a board, light as a feather," if your first thought is, "Am I making my body stiff enough?" rather than, "They might drop me," you probably know how to trust others, but not so much yourself.

Most of us probably know that if we could trust the lesser side of that equation, our life would be more filling, meaningful, and creative. In improv that difference is obvious. The audience might not know why the choices are bland and the scene is going nowhere, but improvisers can spot overly protective behavior in less than a heartbeat because we have all lived the excruciating mediocrity of holding back. We also all know the ridiculous miraculous joy that can happen when everyone lets go of their inhibitions and surrenders completely to the sacred moment of play. That sensation is like breathing for the first time. So we teach ourselves how to trust, and who we can trust

4. Brené Brown, *Dare to Lead* (New York: Random House, 2018), 29–32.

to give us the life for which we are all gasping. Even still, trust is just hard. Trusting others is hard, and it should be, because betrayal is real. Trusting yourself is also hard, and it should be, because self-sabotage is real too.

Trust, like all the skills of improv and spirituality, requires practice. There is something that is handy about an improv class that I think should also be true about church. I say that because both the art of improv and the art of faith depend squarely on our ability to trust.

I will never forget the first time I was in an improv class and they said we were going to do trust games. I like trust games, but I had no idea what I was in for. We played a game called "Blind Run." For this game, you have a long aisle, long enough to run and really get up some speed. You place a volunteer on each side at the end of the aisle. Each of the volunteers reaches their inside arm out like a hook. A contestant at the opposite end of the aisle is blindfolded and spun around. Then they are required to run full speed with both of their arms out in a similar hook. The idea is that when the contestant is at the end of the shoot, his arms will hook those of the volunteers, bringing the contestant to a stop before he hits the wall. Like I said, I like trust games. They usually come easy for me, but I can't tell you what a mind trick it is to make your feet go as fast as they can when you can't see.

That night I was angry at my teacher. We had just met. There is no way to expect that level of trust on night one. I mean, they had just found out I am a priest. How many people would want to see me smack a wall for that alone? Over time, though, I have come to appreciate my teacher's wisdom. When you are improvising, you try to trust your partner and you try to trust yourself, but sometimes you just can't, so you learn to trust the process itself. You learn to have faith in the process, to be all in, whether you are in a state of heart to feel trust in that moment or not. You learn to stop trying to create trust and instead start surrendering. When you are doing that real time in front of a paying audience, it feels like you are running blindfolded at a brick wall. But when players actually succeed at it, it is awesome. It is hilarious, entertaining, and beautiful because **the audience delights to see the moment when trust turns into faith.**

Trust and Faith Are Practices, Not Goalposts

For all I have said about the ridiculously important role that trust and faith play in our personal, creative, social, and societal lives, I also want to point out that neither trust nor faith is ever perfect or complete in this life. Betrayal is real. We see that at the heart of the gospel in so many ways. I mean, there is a reason they call a betrayer a "Judas" after all. Because life for us mortals is a mystery, our trust can never be fully secure; our faith will never become certainty because we will never know if we are having faith in the right things.

In my ordained career, I have had to learn about lost trust quickly. As I mentioned, in my first placement as a priest, the rector (my boss) was removed for misconduct. These kinds of things are difficult to say the least. We know from experience that most of the time when we try to bury the details, they fester over time. Rumors fill the vacuum, and before you know it, the facts lose all meaning.

For that reason, in cases of misconduct the Episcopal Church pivots to an open strategy. We try to come clean about what happened, or at least as clean as possible. In our case, that meant that the bishop sent out a letter telling the whole congregation that my boss had had an ongoing affair for years. Still, for the sake of privacy, the woman's name was not revealed. You can imagine how a church could blow up at that. Many people were angry at my former boss. So many people were angry at the bishop for handling it in such a public way (though she was required to, given the rules of the church). I don't pretend to know what the right thing to do is in that situation, but I got the ministry equivalent of the Thunderdome.

There was one moment I don't think I will ever forget. It was a Sunday and the news had come out by letter the week before. The bishop came to celebrate the Eucharist and preach and have a public forum after the service. The only place big enough to accommodate everyone was the worship space, which was lovely. Every detail was refined, from the stained glass to the Gothic archways, to the six-foot-tall candleholders that framed the altar. It was packed like Easter morning, but no one was there for Peeps or pastels.

The pews were brimming with people in all different stages of grief. The bishop was up front holding her own in the questions and answers, even as we were fiddling with the microphones to make them work. I was standing off to the side. I get antsy when I am stuck in a chair, and I literally didn't know where I was supposed to be. I had been a priest for a month at this point. I found myself standing next to the canon to the ordinary, who is basically the bishop's number two in the diocese.

The microphone in the congregation was brought to a man with his hand up for a question. All the hubbub in the room stopped. This man was one of the biggest givers in the congregation and pretty much everyone knew it. Several of the most exquisite pieces in that beautiful sanctuary held a plaque with his family's name on it. Most people in the congregation also knew that he and his family were very close to the just-removed rector. He took the microphone and stood up. He was tall and commanding. You could tell he was accustomed to being a strong presence in a room.[5]

The previous question had been about what happened next since the rector no longer worked at the church. The bishop said that there would be a discernment process to find the next rector. She explained that would probably take some time, eighteen months to two years, and that she didn't want our congregation to ever have to experience

---

5. That commanding presence was probably a necessity from the kind of business he was in. I had no idea and still have no idea what his job actually was. There is a kind of success that is so intimidating even a pastor is afraid to ask.

misconduct like this again, especially since we already had before.[6] Then the tall man stood up and spoke: "I know I speak for everyone here," he said,[7] "when I say the *last* thing we need is a damned discernment process."

The use of the term "damned" was particularly poignant to me in the worship space. I turned to the canon to the ordinary, and I said, "Wow. We have our work cut out for us."

I was right. And I honestly think we did the work: all of us together, congregation and clergy. It took a long time.

Please don't read this story the wrong way. The man who stood up was caring and generous. How could he place his trust in the bishop when his friend and priest, a man he admired and probably shared his most intimate secrets with, was hurting?

I learned so much from my experience at that church. I even came up with crazy theories on pastoral misconduct, pastoral role, and the "character" of a priest. Most of what I learned there was about trust and how it "spiderwebs" when it breaks. For example, imagine talking to a newlywed couple trying to make sense of the fact that the man who fed them their vows broke his own. Imagine what it might bring up for a couple who had lived through infidelity and had reconciled.

Trust "spiderwebs." It breaks like a windshield hit by a rock. The point of impact is affected, but the cracks spread to unpredictable places. And the longer you drive before you treat it, the more the cracks spread. As a pastor, even a relatively innocent one, there was no way to protect myself from the effects of that spread.

---

6. Interesting fact: most congregations don't experience clergy misconduct, but those that do tend to see it over and over. There are lots of theories out there as to why that is, but we really don't know. Treating the systemic issues in a congregation is more art than science—art like Salvadore Dalí, not like Thomas Kinkade.

7. By the way, if someone, especially someone with power in an organization, says something like "I know I speak for everyone here," you are about to get smacked.

We joke that the reason we wear a white clerical collar is so it can function as a screen on which everyone can project their own personal issues. Whether you are a pastor, a pew-sitting Christian, or a human in the world, you bear the burden of broken trust. A relationship with God makes you even more of a target, because when we are hurt, imagining God's judgment is so much easier than seeing his constant compassion and love.

What do you do with all this trust stuff? If trust is both all-important and unpredictable, how do you live and minister, much less tell a few jokes?

Build up your partner.

There is a famous story among improvisers. An improviser who won an award for the quality of his improv prowess took the podium, held the statue in his hand, looked out at the crowd, and said, "I am so sorry. . . . Improv is an art that is all about making your partner look good. If I have won this, I must have failed. I am really sorry. I will try to do better next time." Then he stepped down from the stage.

Improvisers hold an unwavering commitment to treat their scene partner as absolutely brilliant. This is one of the most important strategies that improvisers use to develop faith and trust. Every joke that fails is just a setup for something that can be brought back later. Every strange choice is an opening to a whole new depth of storyline.

The crazy part is that it works. We are so used to trying to separate ourselves from others' failings (as natural to us as avoiding a leper was in the first century) that we never stop to imagine what would happen if we jumped in. I have seen it, and it is hilarious. I have seen an improviser who (I hate to say, but) was dumber than a bag of hammers, and watched as the person on the stage with him soaked up every word and choice as if it were brilliant. That isn't to say that they substituted their judgment for his, but seeing him be taken seriously, like *seriously*, led to one of the funniest things I have ever witnessed.

Conclusion

This is the comma space, the desert between slavery and promise, the liminal space where we move from merely accepting what is to a place where we can give from ourselves. How long it takes you to make that transition depends on a lot of things, but more than anything else it depends on how much you practice. It took the Israelites in the desert forty years to get over their hurt and choose to trust both God (their partner) and themselves. On stage I have seen that comma last only four milliseconds, but if you could look closely enough, I am sure you would always find it. The choice to trust opens you up to build something together.

Chapter 5

"&"

I fully believe everything I said in the last chapters about the power of "yes," and the sad truth is that saying "yes" alone is no different than saying nothing. Let me show you an example. Imagine a scene:

Player 1: Look at the lilies!

Player 2: Yes, I see them.

Player 1: Aren't they beautiful?

Player 2: Sure are.

Player 1: They remind me of our mother.

Player 2: They do!

Player 1: She always said, "A lily in your hair is better than a gown of the finest silk."

Player 2: She did say that a lot.

Player 1: Too bad she was so allergic.

Player 2: Too bad for sure.

Player 1: We should have known that she would sneeze herself to death.

Player 2: We were caught unaware.

Player 1: The flowers at the funeral were gorgeous, though. Do you remember what they were?

Player 2: . . . I remember they were gorgeous, but no, I don't recall what they were.

Player 1: They were lilies, Matilda. Lilies!

Player 2: Of course!

Notice how player 2 always agreed but never did any of the work of the scene. You see this with beginning improvisers all the time. People learn how to say "yes," but they don't find the courage or fortitude to offer their own unique "&." From Sam Wells's example in chapter 3: if the pianist had stayed on the bench and let the kid play, but had not reached his arm around to add harmony, he might as well have walked away.

If the deacon I talked about in the introduction had just stepped aside and let the young woman read the Gospel, I would have walked away learning, "Sometimes church rules are stupid." That may be true,[1] yet because of the audacity it took to stand silent and extend the stole, I walked away with an image of God that heals me daily—and a sermon illustration that has now lasted over a decade.

An acknowledging "yes" without working together is merely a softer version of rejection. How many romantic comedies have poked at the awkwardness of one person saying for the first time, "I love you," and the other person answering, "Cool"?

That is why I don't like the phrase "nonanxious presence" in pastoral care. It is also why I was terrible on stage for my first five years improvising. I thought supporting my partner just meant getting out of the way of what they had in mind. What I never stopped to think about was how that put all the pressure on my partner. The reality is that making a choice to add something to the world is the way you support your partner. Therefore, in improv any choice that you make is called a "gift." The gift may not be something desirable, but it is a

---

1. If you are reading this, sorry, Bishop.

gift because it offers your partner something to work off of. The right gift—the right "&"—can bring together things that were in tension.

Relapse Is Part of Recovery

Once I was doing premarital counseling with a couple. Neither of them had had an easy life up to that point, and the woman had dealt with some serious addiction issues. The man had known her then, so he had seen how bad it could get, but she had been sober for years. While her addiction issues had been mentioned in previous sessions, they didn't appear to be a current problem in their relationship.

One day the couple came into my office for our scheduled appointment and I could see something was wrong. They kept a greater physical distance from each other. The woman looked upset. The man looked like he was in shock. Eventually, I got the woman to explain what happened. She had been so badly triggered earlier in the day that she stopped at a liquor store, bought a bottle of peach schnapps, and took a swig. Then she stopped, put the top on the bottle, and hid it under her car seat. She kept repeating, "I don't know why I stopped. I don't know why I stopped. I guess I just didn't like the taste." She repeated that script like it was a record playing on a broken turntable, the saddest part of a sad song stuck on continuous repeat. In between those repeats, she let me know that her fiancé had found the partially drunk bottle under her car seat.

I asked the man what he was thinking, and he explained that he couldn't get over the thought that her addiction would always be looming over them. He had lost hope of real recovery for his fiancée; the distance in his body and his despondent face pierced my heart like the sound of a bugle playing taps.

I knew what they say about addiction: "Relapse is part of recovery." I also know that relapse is the worst nightmare of the one who loves an alcoholic. There is often a wave of support around those who get sober the first time. After that, things can change quickly.

At first, I said all of the things you might expect a priest to say. I told her that she wasn't alone (yes) and that we would make sure that she got treatment because her sobriety was precious. She kept coming back to the same script.

"I don't know why I stopped." She understood why she drank. She understood why her fiancé was despondent, but what mystified her was why she stopped after one drink. That kind of incongruous detail is what improv training makes you notice. It has been said that a novice improviser is trying to decide what will happen, and an experienced improviser sees that it already is. Theologically, I think that is another way to say that the Holy Spirit is at work. God is already healing all of those surrounding us. Those kinds of details are often signs that healing is beginning to manifest. Believing that God is already involved makes being a Christian much easier.

"Why did you stop?" I asked her.

She repeated the same thing: "I guess I just didn't like the taste."

I did something unexpected, but true to myself. I haven't had as close experience with addiction as some, but this wasn't my first time looking the demonic illness in the face. I knew of alcoholics who drank Old Spice when other liquor wasn't available, and she knew that the reason she stopped didn't have to do with taste, or she wouldn't have been stuck on repeat.

She said it again. "I guess I just didn't like the taste."

"That is bullshit," I said, aware that I was in my clerical collar and suit and I was breaking the norms of the situation. But it worked. They both stopped looking at the floor for the first time. They looked at me.

"That is bullshit." I reiterated. "You're an alcoholic. You don't care about taste." She nodded. "Why did you stop?"

"Because I was ashamed," she blurted as the tears began falling even faster.

I offered some kind words and let the room calm down a little. But I knew I wasn't done. The man was still at a distance. His question hadn't been answered yet. He still didn't know how he could find it in himself to trust again. Then came the real "&" I had to offer. I looked at the woman and said, "While I know that you are feeling terrible right now, I also want you to know that I believe what happened today was *progress*."

"What?" she said with genuine shock and confusion.

I replied, "You said the reason you stopped drinking was because you were ashamed, right?"

"Yes," she said, looking at the floor again.

"Well, what did you used to do when you were ashamed?"

"Drink," she said with a nod and half a chuckle.

"See," I said, "that is progress." The man leaned forward for the first time and held her hand.

This is an "&" in the improv sense because it took the couple's struggle and built off of it. She was stuck. They were stuck. Yes, she drank. Yes, that was scary, and in this story there was progress. I thought about taking the swearing out of the story, but I left it in because from my perspective it was part of the "&." It shocked their systems enough to know that I was really in the room with them, because it was surprising and outside of their expectation. At that point I was no longer just "the nice pastor": I claimed my place in the room and insisted that I had an unexpected gift to give. I shocked the woman out of her head so that we could build something together.

Crown upon Your Head and Justification

"&" is a powerful tool. Here is an example of a specific kind of "&" called a "justification." I was called to meet a man I had never met before. He didn't go to my church, but he was a relative of someone who did. He was elderly, but had remained quick, spry, and healthy into his old age. He lived in another state and had fallen and broken his hip while he was visiting. That kind of injury can cause an older person to quickly spiral downward physically. If one problem leads to another, it can lead to death.

I went to visit him and we had a long chat. He said he had always been a religious man, but church had not been part of his life. He said he had played football in college, and he talked about how he had raised sons and was now a grandfather. He was clearly a proud man—not in a bad way, just in the sense that he was self-reliant and that he enjoyed using his strength and ability to support and protect the people in his life. He talked about how he had always been healthy. He was recovering from surgery for the first time. He had never even been in a hospital before the accident. Though he easily had four decades on me, I have been sick most of my life, so I told him a little about my experiences and illnesses. We talked about Peter after the Last Supper and how he tried to stop Jesus from washing his feet. We talked about how loving doesn't just mean giving care; it also means receiving it.

It isn't uncommon for people to get stuck in the same thought circles, especially when they are facing mortality. The man kept making reference to a poem. I didn't understand how it connected, but he kept bringing it up.

"When you are born," he would say, "God puts a crown upon your head. From time to time, it falls off. When it does, you do the right thing and put it back on again."

He told me about the poem. Five minutes later, he brought it up again and said that he had sent it to his grandchildren. I couldn't tell if he wrote the poem or was quoting it. I wasn't even sure it sounded like a poem. I thought it might be a prelude to a confession. "From time to time the crown falls off" sounded to me like guilt over a moral failure. I kept fishing for that, but he didn't bite.

After a while of back-and-forth, I began to wonder if the crown wasn't something simpler to him. He seemed so depressed over his weakness. It is not uncommon for a health crisis to cause a vocational one too. People can have trouble seeing purpose in their life if they are cut off from those things that they think they do well.

I asked him a couple times, "What does that mean, 'the crown falls from your head'?" but either he didn't have the language for what it meant, or I didn't understand. So I asked again in a slightly different way, "When the crown falls from your head, is that weakness? Do you feel like the crown has fallen because you can't walk right now?" He said, "Yes." I began to see from his perspective and share his reality for a while. My intuition wasn't wrong. He saw his own weakness as a moral failing, but he didn't think weakness in others was failure.

We talked more about weakness. I told him that I wondered how weakness could be a sin if it was so much of Christ's life and especially death. After a long conversation I left and he seemed a little lighter. His family told me that our meeting meant a lot to him, and we met again. Eventually, though, he took a quick turn for the worse and I was called out to do last rites.

Last rites weren't designed to be about death. The technical term for it is "extreme unction," which is a service for healing with an anointing. But over the years the church has learned that there is often a pastoral need to have a way of saying goodbye and entrusting our loved ones over to God. Perhaps because of its history, I always look to last rites not just as a ritual, but an invitation to spiritual healing for both the dying and the grieving.

I have a practice of adding something to the service of last rites. There is a powerful prayer, the Prayer of Commendation, where we as a community give the person we love over to God's care. The words are so heavy that I am often concerned it will take the family by surprise. I wonder if they know what they are asking for when they ask for last rites. Here are the words of that prayer:

> Depart, O Christian soul, out of this world;
> In the Name of God the Father Almighty who created
>   you;
> In the Name of Jesus Christ who redeemed you;

> In the Name of the Holy Spirit who sanctifies you.
> May your rest be this day in peace,
> And your dwelling place in the Paradise of God.
>   (BCP, 464)

You can understand my hesitation. I basically order the person to die, which is actually a gift. When death is imminent, the people around are usually holding on to life tightly. They need to be told it is not just okay to let go, it is right to let go. I especially want to prepare the family because I don't want them to miss the tenderness of the next prayer.

> Into your hands, O merciful Savior, we commend your servant (name). Acknowledge, we humbly beseech you, a sheep of your own fold, a lamb of your own flock, a sinner of your own redeeming. Receive *him* into the arms of your mercy, into the blessed rest of everlasting peace, and into the glorious company of the saints in light. (BCP, 465)

To prepare a family for that powerful moment, I make it my practice not only to explain before the service what will happen, but I add some time right before that prayer for them to say some final goodbyes. To cut the awkwardness of the silence during that time, I usually step back and sing "Amazing Grace." It adds to the intimacy of the moment, and also gives them a cue that it is time to say their final goodbyes.

After this particular family said their goodbyes, I bent over to speak directly to the man: "When you were born, God put a crown upon your head. Every time it fell off, you did the right and honorable thing and picked it back up and put it on your head. It is about to fall one last time. But that is okay, because this time Christ will pick it up and put it on your head, and it will never fall again. It will never fall again."

A justification in improv is when you use your space to make things that seem like they won't go together go together. Justification is also a technical term in theology, and you can have a lot of fun playing at the intersection, but you can see the importance of the intersection in this story. This man was stuck. For him, weakness equaled failure of dignity. Whether or not he could make sense of the words I said, I restored dignity to his death while respecting his worldview—two things that shouldn't have worked together suddenly did. This is a remarkable skill for soul care, and the creativity it takes comes more and more naturally with practice.

Finding the Words

When I first became a priest I never imagined I would find words like that. The truth is, I still don't think that I make them up. I believe that the Holy Spirit, God's very presence, gives us the words, or the silence we need to offer. Just saying that, however, doesn't help us get better at recognizing and welcoming the presence of the Spirit. Just saying, "Get out of the way" doesn't teach us to recognize, much less trust, the immense courage and fierceness of those holy moments when souls are on the line.

This is why cultivating the practice of "&" is an invaluable part of spiritual formation for the Christian life. Many pastoral care professors talk about the ministry of presence. They are right: being there is more important than what you say. But just being in the room isn't in and of itself healing. The practice of "&" helps us be deeply present rather than just standing there. It teaches us to trust our instincts so that we know when the Spirit is whispering in our ear.

This is true for the Christian because it is true of God too. I believe that one of the reasons why teaching and training people in ministry can be so difficult is because many of us, especially in mainline American Christianity, have lost all expectations of God's active presence in our world in any true sense. Anyone who has studied American colonial history can tell you about Deism. Many of the founders of our country were Christian in name, but what they actually believed was that God set the world in motion and then left it to us. Sometimes this idea is referred to as the "clockmaker God" theology. A clockmaker makes the clock and then lets it run. A clock-maker might return to repair it if broken, but that is about it.

That is not Christianity. We believe that God is present and active in our lives at every moment in the form of the Holy Spirit. Pentecost marks the birth of the church because it gives direct access to God for all believers. Many pastors (including myself) know too well that the all-consuming fire of the Spirit has little to do with what most church-goers believe. For many, church has become a place of denial—a place that tells us what we are supposed to be like, or worse, what we are supposed to pretend to be like. For some, it is a place of "yes"—a place where we are accepted and forgiven and told to go and sin no more.

Without "&," however, "yes" isn't incarnation. It's Deism. God becomes just a clockmaker or a rule-maker or the Santa Claus of prayers. In my experience, most self-identified Christians think of God in one of these three ways, but none of them can be honestly rec-tified with Jesus's pattern of life much less his teaching.

Think about the parables and similes Jesus uses for the kingdom of God. It is like a pearl of such value you would sell everything you own just to buy it.[2] It is like a hidden treasure that you would trade anything for.[3] It is like the leaven in the bread which transforms the whole loaf.[4] It is the mustard seed that grows.[5] The idea that God is active and involved in our world is an indispensable part of authentic Christianity.

Let's go back to the parable of the good Samaritan. As I men-tioned before, that story was scandalous because it revealed the racial

2. Matthew 13:45–46
3. Matthew 13:44
4. Matthew 13:33
5. Matthew 13:31–32

and religious tensions between Jews and Samaritans. It also creates a caricature of how worthless removed faith can be. Remember when the priest and the Levite avoided the man in the ditch? That would not have been surprising to Jesus's audience. They were both upright religious people. The priest had to be ritually clean to do his job. Touching blood ritually defiled a person, which meant that helping the bloody man would have precluded the priest from doing his job that day. The priest was too holy to get in the ditch, but Jesus turned holiness upside down. Jesus's unique "&" held the Samaritan as an example of neighborly ministry. The "good one" in the story is the one who got in the ditch with the beaten man; so it is with God, according to Jesus.

"God is doing something" is the thesis statement of the New Testament. Put another way, God is giving an "&." One of the reasons improv is thrilling and scary to do is that you can't control it. The scene is alive because you can never fully predict your partner. That is also what faith is like with a living God. In improv you share a scene with your partner, lose control, and find beauty. In faith we find a living God, lose control, and find our redemption.

Exercise: A, C, What's the B?

This exercise is designed to help you not only find an "&," but also prepare your mind to find justifications in the improv sense. On the next page are sets of two words. Make up something that joins them together. Write the first thing, a single connecting word, that comes to mind clearly and try to do it as quickly as possible. There is no right or wrong. It can be seemingly random—"seemingly" because they will be connected even if their connection is not obvious to your conscious mind. You are teaching yourself to trust your intuition, and developing the specific creative improv sense of justification: when you take two things that don't seem to go together and discover how they actually fit. In improv, justification is what makes the scenes feel miraculous and hysterical. It is also the most basic skill of missional ministry since missional ministry begins with seeing what is already on the ground and how it connects to the gospel. Missional ministry starts with the "yes" of radical acceptance of both what is and what is missing. Combining those things into something meaningful is the work of "&."

Rabbit _____ France

Book _____ Prison

Pen _____ Funeral

Tree _____ Dog

Flower _____ Breakup

Coffin _____ Sneeze

Church _____ Criminal

Work _____ Play

Stop _____ Time

Take a moment and look over what you wrote. Were some of the connections easy? Were some hard? Looking back, can you now see what connected some of the three-word strands better than when you first wrote them? •

"&" and the Technical Improv Skill

Doing anything and making any choice following a "yes" is technically an "&" in improv, and improvisers work hard to try to hone their intuition and reflexes around it. While there are some varied ways of understanding it, from my study and practice it generally goes like this: you want to be able to be free to let your mind make new connections and you also want there to be a gravity toward working with your scene partners. You want your "&" to flow from their "yes." Sometimes this is called "building up, not out." Imagine the following scene:

Player A: Let's go to the zoo.

Player B: Yes! I would love to see the penguins.

Player A: And the giraffes.

Player B: Ooh—and we can eat cotton candy.

Player A: Then we could go to the movies.

Player B: And for a beautiful Sunday drive.

All of that was "Yes, &"—technically. They were sharing the same reality. They were positive. And nothing happened because they kept changing the subject from line to line. Now look at this variation:

Player A: Let's go to the zoo.

Player B: Yes! I would love to see the penguins.

Player A: I know. They are so fancy. They look like they are wearing tuxedos.

Player B: Hey, let's go into this tuxedo shop, and we can sneak in with the penguins.

Player A: That sounds awesome, Frankie, but I'm scared 'cause I don't know how to swim.

Player B: I will hold your hand.

Player A: You would, Frankie? Well, if we are already going to be holding hands and wearing tuxes, why don't we just get married while we are at it?

Player B: Hmmm. I mean, this seems a little fast for a first date, but the zoo is a beautiful place for a wedding. I'm in.

Player A: Yay!

Player B: I just hope I don't get confused and marry a penguin instead.

Player A: Oh yeah—they mate for life.

You see how the second scene is richer and fuller? We even got one of their names. We know that they are on a first date, so we know something about their relationship. We also know their world is a little sideways. People could get confused, marry a penguin, and then be stuck.

The "&" Model of Discernment

As a priest (and as a person), something I talk a lot about is people finding God's call. I deeply believe that God has a call, or a place, or a way that people can use their unique gifts for the good of the kingdom. It looks different for every person. I also believe that it changes from season to season in a person's life. One of the things that can be daunting for people when they try to think about finding their call is that it can be overwhelming. There are too many choices, too many possibilities. When we fall deeply in love with God, there is often a yearning to do something so radical that there is no foreseeable way to get from point A to B. This is where the build-up-not-out process is helpful.

One life-changing thing for my ministry was when I attended an Appreciative Inquiry training.[6] I learned many tools for ministry from that training that I use at least monthly. One of the brilliant things that they do is get people to talk about some of their best or favorite experiences in ministry. Before we proceed, let's do that.

Exercise: Best Experience

. . . .

Think of a few times in ministry or worship when you felt completely alive. Name and explain three of those best experiences below. Put not only the name of the thing, but what you appreciated most about it, and what your part was in making it happen.

1. _____

2. _____

3. _____

---

6. I highly recommend their resources, and you can find out more about them at appreciativeway.com.

Now look for themes. What connects these experiences? What makes one of them stand out from the others? •

Whether I am doing this myself, or interviewing someone else about their experiences, I find doing these kinds of exercises to be fun. We love to talk about what we love. Here is the brilliant part: whatever it was that connected those experiences, or whatever it was that made one stand out, those are your values. People and organizations waste hours on painstakingly boring work to try to identify their core values, but when you act out of your values, you feel most alive. Your best experiences are your best because you were living your values. So go in the back door. Talk about what brought joy and fun and life and fulfillment. That is you "yes"-ing yourself; then have the courage to clarify by saying, "and the reason I loved that so much is because I care about _____."

Frederick Buechner famously wrote, "Your vocation in life is where your greatest joy meets the world's greatest need."[7] That makes sense to me. What doesn't make sense to me is how much energy people spend researching the world's greatest need and so little time researching their greatest joy. Some of Jesus's parting words in the Gospel of John are, "If you keep my commandments, you will abide in my love, just as I have kept my Father's commandments and abide in his love. I have said these things to you so that my joy may be in you, and that your joy may be complete. This is my commandment, that you love one another as I have loved you" (John 15:10–12). Jesus tells us that his commandments exist so that our joy might be complete. This is significant. How can we be people of Jesus unless we are serious about what our joy really is? Yet so often we think of holiness as a badge we wear when it is really supposed to be part of who we are.

---

7. Frederick Buechner, *Wishful Thinking: A Seeker's ABC* (San Francisco, CA: HaperSanFrancisco, 1993), 118–19.

"&" and Formation: Staking a Tomato Plant

Accepting holiness as a part of who we are is not something that comes easily. Once I asked a young man in my church if he wanted to be an acolyte (altar server). He said "no" because he didn't feel worthy to wear the robes. I wish I had had some great way of handling that, but I didn't. The truth is, we struggle with worthiness all the time in ministry. I wanted to tell him, "I feed you the body and blood of Christ every week. How could you be unworthy to wear a white dress?" I wanted to tell him what I deeply know, which is that if we only let the worthy serve on the altar there would be a bunch of empty robes and no one to speak the prayers. Of course, he wasn't the only one. I can relate. I still don't know what God was thinking when he called me of all people to be a priest. I remind God quite often that this was God's idea, not mine.

The truth is our best ministry comes from who we are, not in spite of who we are. When I was in seminary, I had a bit of a vocational crisis. I like to think of myself as an innovator, and some frustrations led me to believe that isn't what the Episcopal Church really wanted. A good friend stopped me by asking, "Why would you let 'those people' define your priesthood?" I thought more about it and I realized that I had been looking at my seminary experience wrong. If you had asked me, I would have told you the right thing: I was a unique person and being human is a prerequisite to being a priest, so my individuality would shine through in my ministry. But one of the things we learn about in pastoral care is that people have latent beliefs. We have thoughts or beliefs about God or the world that live under the surface of our mind. They guide us even though we are unaware of them.

My latent belief was that I went to seminary so that I could be melted down and cast into the image of a priest. Not only was that idea unhelpful, it was also idolatrous, but there it was. In a real sense I thought the work I was doing was not to improve me but to turn me into something I was not.

One of the problems with latent beliefs is that they are hard to get out of your head. So much so that telling yourself not to believe them rarely helps. It is often a better strategy to replace the thought with another or with an image that moves you closer to your truer path. I found the image of staking a tomato plant. You stake a tomato plant so it doesn't collapse under its own weight. That way it can be more of what it is and produce more fruit. That is how I have thought about spiritual study and learning ever since. Seminary was the stake for my tomato plant, not the means for replacing my broken self.

Exercise: "Yes, &"

This exercise is best done with a partner, but if you are by yourself, you can do it with some props. Get two simple objects: maybe two keys, or a clothespin and a fork. Whatever they are doesn't matter, but eventually they will work a little like your puppets. Each one of them will play a character. If you are doing this with a partner, sit across from each other, as each of you will play a character.

I want the two characters to have a discussion about something. After the first one says something, every line should start with the word "yes" followed by a summary of the previous statement, then the word "and" followed by something new. Go for a few lines or till you hit a high point, then call the scene and try a new one.

For example:

Player A: I bought a truck today.

Player B: Yes, you bought a truck today, and you will let me borrow it.

Player A: Yes, I will let you borrow it, and I want you to only use it for family business.

Player B: Yes, I will only use it for family business, and since we are lumberjacks that is perfect.

Player A: Yes, we are lumberjacks, so trucks are important, and that is why I am letting you use it at all since you wrecked my last one.

Player B: Yes, I wrecked the last one, and I still blame the advertising. How is Ford supposed to be tough if it can't even take a tree?

Now you try it. I will give you the suggestion: Walkie-talkie.

Now try it again with aluminum foil.

Now bald eagle.

Write notes about what you noticed. How did it feel for you? What were your favorite moments? Did anything make you laugh out loud? Did you or your partner have trouble keeping the directions? Did people start saying "no"? Or "yes, but"? Were you able to build up, or did you find yourself building out?

If you had trouble keeping to the directions, don't feel bad. I do this exercise with a lot of people, and every time a few of them really get tripped up. It is really interesting to see how even generally positive people can be pulled into a combative mindset without realizing it. If you did have trouble with it, keep practicing, and keep noticing what leads you to falter and what it feels like when both characters are building the other up. •

Chapter 6

Mime and Mystery, Rules and Freedom

A Quick Recap

By now you have a basic understanding of "Yes, &," the process in improv where we agree to the reality that is being offered and build off of it together. Hopefully, you are beginning to (re)train your brain to form authentic and positive connections with people and you are beginning to see how the grace of God is manifest in Christianity through the lens of loving collaboration.

There is a common debate among improvisers. Many teach the "rules of improv," but others say the only rule of improv is that there are no rules. I like to think that if there was more crossover with the monastic tradition that debate would end. So right here, today, this improv priest will put it to rest.

"Yes, &" isn't a rule of improv in the way most people think about rules. It isn't a stop sign, or a notice to stay off the grass. "Yes, &" is a rule of life. A "rule of life" is a term used most often in the Christian monastic tradition to describe the life-giving practices that we keep to sustain us at our best. Every monastic order has one, with the Rule of St. Benedict probably the most famous. Benedict's rule includes all kinds of things, from how many times a day you worship to how you deal with conflict to how you think about doing the dishes. To most of us today, Benedict's rule with its eight distinct prayer times a day starting at midnight (followed by a 3:00 a.m.—oof) seems onerous, but it is important to remember that the popularity of Benedict's rule was largely due to how much more relaxed it was compared to other monastic rules that preceded it. Today, many Christian communities or just individual Christians have their own rule of life. When I teach about it, I often talk about how hard it is for contemporary Christians to wrap their head around that name because we hear "RULE of life," but what we really should hear is "rule OF LIFE." Prayer, service, evangelism, or even doing the dishes can be opportunities for union with God. They are the stakes in our tomato plants. They are the rules of life that open us up to the communal creativity, grace, discovery, and joy that define the artform, whether we are talking about improv or life.

The Irony of Creativity

Hopefully, you are beginning to put together that creativity itself is not what most people think. We talk about creativity as if you are making something. But what improv has taught me is that if you want to be truly creative, funny, or graceful, you must think about creativity not as a process of creation but rather one of discovery. "Yes, &" is not a plan. It is a process for discovery.

There is a legend which says that someone once asked Michelangelo how he sculpted a masterwork like *David*. He responded, "It is simple. The figure is already in the marble. You just have to chip away the extra bits." Put another way, **the artist makes nothing, but discovers everything.**

Most people don't think of art that way. They think of art as a process of vision then implementation. Vision and implementation are skills that are useful in a variety of ways, but they will never set the soul free. To make true art (or ministry, for that matter), you have to make the space for inspiration to come from outside of your head. It is our connection to the mystical that makes for great art and even greater religion. This is why discovery is a core part of the artist's rule of life. It is discovery because we are tapped into something larger than our imagination or process. True art cannot be made using a paint-by-number method. The artist can't focus on the rules of the craft solely; the discovery comes from opening yourself to act as if something is happening that is greater than your understanding. The artist and the sage are constantly trying to use their craft to better understand the life force beneath everything.

This is one of the fundamental reasons why the artist's journey and the sage's journey intertwine like a Celtic knot. They both require a deep appreciation for mystery. All the greats of Christian spirituality were in love not just with the God they understood, but also with the mystery of God beyond our understanding. Later in the book I will talk about how in America we have misunderstood faith as certainty. Faith is many things, but it is certainly not certainty. Where there is certainty, there is no room for mystery. Where there is no room for mystery, there is no room for God.[1]

One of the most powerful ways improvisers forge this practice of discovery is through mime. On the surface, mime is important for improvisers because we literally have no idea what props we will need beforehand, but there is a deeper purpose for miming in improv: it both paradoxically grounds the play in the physical and teaches the improviser to focus on discovery rather than creation.

There is a lovely novel about improv, *Process: An Improviser's Journey*.[2] The authors were trying to write a book about improv and it wasn't working, so they wrote a novel about a group of friends taking their improv class. I think this is an ingenious way to teach improv. There is one scene in the book where the improv teacher is

---

1. Though you can squeeze in an idol or two.
2. Mary Scruggs and Michael J. Gellman, *Process: An Improviser's Journey* (Evanston, IL: Northwestern University Press, 2008).

auditioning students for entry into the class. He has everyone sit on a chair. Then they reach under their chair and pick up something via mime. The teacher explains to them that they are not supposed to think of the object first. They are supposed to see it, then emotionally react to it. It is difficult to explain the difference between creating an idea in mime versus reaching out and discovering this imaginary thing. It is funny, the way I remember this scene is different and way more frustrating and dramatic from what the book actually says. I read this book ten years ago, and I spent a decade thinking it went like this: the teacher in the story keeps telling the lead character he is doing it wrong and to try again . . . and again and again. Meanwhile the teacher praises other students for doing it right. Finally the main character gets so frustrated he lets go, and sure enough discovers the mime rather than creating it. The teacher notices instantly and tells him that he did a good job.

After recently rereading the book, I discovered there is not a back-and-forth. The student does it the wrong way (by creating an idea), then is corrected and does it the right way (through discovery) the second time.[3] Ask me about this at a party and I will swear the words have rearranged themselves over the last decade, but more likely it is my own projection on the past. Discovery is a hard lesson to learn. I remember failing and failing and failing to get it. I remember how vulnerable it felt to try to create and how miraculous it was to learn to discover instead. Discovery is hard to master, but it is critical to the spirituality of creativity.

The concept of discovery in mime is more than a little mind-bendy. When I first read *Process*, I thought it was nuts. Then one day I was playing this scene where I was an assistant to a mad scientist. My boss asked for a rat to test the thing he was making. I mimed picking up a paper bag, reaching in, and holding the rat by its tail. I remember thinking to myself, "Is it a live rat? Or is it dead? I need to decide."

---

3. Scruggs and Gellman, 23–24.

But as I was looking up into thin air imagining the rat between my character's fingers, stuck in indecision as to whether to make it alive or dead, something shocking happened to me. All of a sudden, I saw the rat that I was imagining, and it was *twitching*. Now was that created by my mind in the scientific sense? Sure. But my encounter with it was not one of creation (making a decision), but rather discovery from the freedom of the moment. Thinking about it still creeps me out because the mime rat got too real for my comfort. It still makes me want to jump—which is a good thing. It is me emotionally reacting to what I am discovering through play. Doing that enough teaches a person to embrace mystery, which is a prerequisite to meeting God and not just our graven image of Him.

Exercise: Mime Blob

Chances are the exercises so far have made you feel a little dumb. That is good. All learning, creativity, mystery, ministry, and connection take place in the awkward zone. Take a breath because if you do this next one right, it will feel even more awkward than the others.

This exercise uses mime. While making fun of mime is one of America's favorite pastimes, mime is actually extremely helpful for unlocking a missional perspective. Improvisers have long known that much more creative power exists in the body than in the mind. It is counterintuitive, but the play of improv is about listening deeply to your body and to your partner, and then bypassing the critical perfectionist parts of the mind so that we can give up trying to create the thing and let ourselves *discover* it.

The other thing that is important about mime is that it teaches you to commit to the imagined reality. You shouldn't just put your hand in the shape it would be to hold a cup of water; you want to tighten your muscles so it feels like the cup is there. This skill of committing to the imagined reality over the reality that the world gives can be an invaluable tool in missional ministry.

Here is the exercise: mime a ball of energy in your hand. The ball is malleable. You can play with it, tug at it, and turn it into anything. Or even better, you can play with it until you discover it becomes something. Maybe a baseball bat, or a top hat. Simply play with the energy ball until it turns into an imaginary something. When you discover what it is, recognize it and then crumple it into an energy ball again. This takes patience, focus, and commitment. Make five different things using this process. Try to let your movements show you what the thing becomes rather than thinking of something in your head before you do it. •

A Counterpoint or an "&"; I'm Not Sure

I have been claiming that "Yes, &" is not a rule of improv but rather a manner of life or "rule of life" in the monastic sense. There is one improv teacher and author who pushes back even more forcefully on this idea of rules, and his work is worth considering both for the improviser and for the Christian. He questions whether all "rules" in improv are designed to take the freedom, mystery, and vulnerability out and, therefore, remove the brilliance too. This perspective opens the door to understand the seeming contradiction between law and freedom that we get from the Bible and highlights a huge temptation in institutions that often unwittingly stifle creativity and performance in the name of risk management.

In his book *Improvise: Scene from the Inside Out*,[4] Mick Napier challenges the rule-based approach to teaching improv in a rather ingenious way. He writes a creation myth for improv. At this point, it is important for me to point out that the rule-based approach to teaching improv contains much more than "Yes, &." It also teaches students (at least in the beginning) not to ask questions, do teaching

---

4. Mick Napier, *Improvise: Scene from the Inside Out* (Portsmouth, NH: Heinemann, 2004).

scenes, negotiate, or talk about what you are doing—and that is just the beginning of the list.

Napier goes on to argue that adherence to these rules does not produce a good scene. He says that we saw bad scenes, noticed things in common, and then made rules against them. Napier argues that the problem isn't asking questions or teaching scenes or disobedience to any of the other rules. The problem is protective behavior on the part of the improviser. If you ask, "What are you doing?" because you don't know what to say and want to move the attention away from yourself, that leads to a floundering scene because you are avoiding making a choice, and you aren't really "&"-ing at all. On the other hand, if your partner says, "I am leaving," and you say, "Why don't you love me anymore?" the question offers a strong choice that will lead to an interesting scene.

I bring all this up because of Paul. In his letters, the relationship between the law and freedom can seem confusing. Paul talks about freedom a lot and it is important to him, but in some of his letters (e.g., 1 Corinthians) it seems like he thinks his congregants are taking him too literally. Yes, in Jesus we are forgiven, he tries to explain, but some of the stuff you are doing is just gross. Nothing is against the rules, but that doesn't mean that everything is good for you.[5]

He creates a beautiful parallel. "Don't steal" is a good rule, but it doesn't work unless it points to how to love your neighbor. I think organizations limit themselves by making a rule against something just because they had a bad experience, even if the rule doesn't truly serve the organization. I once worked in a church where the soundboard was run by volunteers. The volunteers were lovely and committed people, but they didn't know how to use the equipment. Once in a while we would have community groups use the space, and often the volunteers would come to church on Sunday and find that the board wasn't working right. There was a real push to make a rule that

---

5. 1 Corinthians 10:23

no outside group should use the board so that it could stay set. That sounded reasonable, but it concealed the real problem: the volunteers didn't know how to use the equipment. In fact, they complained about the group messing with it on weeks where the church had been completely empty. You can make a rule of "Don't touch the soundboard," or you can do the hard work of learning how to use the equipment.

Paul is trying to teach people the hard lesson to make everything they do a reflection of their faith in Jesus Christ rather than the accumulation of petty desires. That is very different from following a set of rules. It is about complete transformation, not just an amended behavioral contract.

Conclusion

Welcome to the gospel as I believe it has always been: not a behavioral contract, but an invitation to grow along the trellis to meet the source of all creativity and life. I can't tell you how hilarious it is to me that after the years I have spent in church and seminary, I finally learned what God's grace is like with a bunch of people who literally didn't know what they were doing.

As I said before, as a rule of life "Yes, &" is the foundation of all improv; I would argue that more advanced improv techniques are just means of clarifying and sharpening that one phrase. That being said, many of those techniques are helpful for the improviser, and integrating some of these lessons into our practice of Christianity can lead us both as individuals and as a community into deeper union with God through the practice of what is truly a godly character.

Introduction to
Sections II and III

Now you have the basics of improv and hopefully you are beginning to see how they integrate with Christian theology. That's great, and the reason I am writing this book is deeper than that. I believe that, as Christians, we have lost ourselves more than a little. The next two sections look at how we can find ourselves again. I had a problem deciding the order of these next sections.

One of these sections is on returning to our purpose at an individual level. We are called to make disciples, but in our metrics, analysis, and strategy we have often replaced that mission with a mission to either keep the institution alive or, worse, just get more people to wear the label "Christian," which is a shallow substitute for our faith as it is described in the Bible. Creating a shallow substitute for Christianity eclipses true Christianity from the view of the wider community, making it difficult to explain what a Christian is. What is a disciple after all? Would we even know one if we met one? We as a church need to get clear about our purpose and what we are looking to give and do for people beyond just being nice. The other section is about community. What kind of leadership and practices does a community need to produce a true disciple? If we know what we are looking for, then we know what kind of community to make.

The most logical way to proceed appears to be to define discipleship and then talk about how to create a community of discipleship, but I am inverting the order because, in my own experience of faith, understandings have not come in that rational order. We experience life-giving community, and from that we learn and become who we were meant to be as disciples. Jesus didn't give us a ten-step guide to being disciples; he invited people to live, eat, walk, and be perplexed with him, and that is how they learned God's way.[1]

So I offer a backwards book for us backwards people. Section II is about adapting the practices of improv to Christian leadership, specifically increasing the use of collaborative teamwork over specialized teamwork. As I learned to implement these strategies in my own life and congregation, I discovered something completely unplanned. I found that with this kind of grace-filled community we start making true disciples. As I said before, no one has ever been brilliant or beautiful without someone first telling them that they are. We can only find the kind of discipleship that the scriptures are talking about through the experience of a loving, creative, and empowering community. At least, that is the only way I know how to do it.

Section III is about discipleship itself—the qualities and mix of virtues it takes to identify and define it. While I will offer many ideas, I will not define the list of qualities for you. Instead, I will lead you through a process where you will come up with a definition for discipleship as *you* see it. I believe the church needs more conversation about discipleship rather than some half-cocked improv priest telling you what you should or should not care about.

Disclaimer: If you work in church administration in any way (clergy or professional layperson), the discussion of church leadership

---

1. Arguably we did get a ten-step guide in the commandments. But that proves my point. The guide didn't get us where we need to be. Sharing our life with God is what is necessary to teach the graceful way.

may seem frustrating because leading this way seems inefficient. It *is* inefficient. Making true disciples is inefficient work. It is slow and painful, and it is a path full of betrayal just like Jesus told us it would be. And once you find this path, you also realize that it is infinitely fun. Hang in there with me, even if it seems like this book lacks an endgame. Every great improv scene feels that way until we discover the purpose together in the end.

SECTION

Fostering a Grace-Filled Community

Chapter 7

Let Play Be the Teacher

Play is the best teacher I know. Think about how many learning strategies involve games or creating games. Think about how much easier it is to learn the periodic table of elements if you make it into a song. Despite our cultural obsession with work, play will out-efficient work every time. Put on some music and cleaning will go faster. Experiment with some new ingredients and dinner will pop.

I never truly appreciated the power and importance of play until I had kids. Watching a child discover the world is a mystifying thing. From a game of peek-a-boo to trading smiles, the playful wonder of a child is infectious. I am not just sentimentalizing childhood innocence. Babies know something we forget, and that is how to prioritize play. Play isn't just wasting time. Play is how we learn to be human and about the world around us. Having children will throw your anxiety into overdrive because they will touch, lick, and suck anything. That is because they are playing with their environment. The game is discovery, and it is how we get to know everything we know.

I find it interesting that I never taught my sons how to play. I have taught them plenty of skills. I have taught them games with rules. I have taught them to buckle down, focus, and work, but I never taught them to play. They just knew. Play is the most ingenious unspoken instinct. I believe it was the playful spark of curiosity that led to the discovery of fire. I believe that a bunch of cave boys and girls were playing "throw a rock down the hill" when one of them thought for the first time, "Hey, wheel." And I believe that play itself is one of the most precious gifts from God. It is given for our thriving. Knowing that God is the great Creator even makes me wonder if play is an essential part of God's image.

There are tons of books on improv, but I know of no teacher that suggests trading performance time for reading time. Play is the true teacher. Words can guide or soothe or polish, but we never know something until we play it.

This makes intuitive sense if you let it. There are some things that you have to experience to believe: parenthood, for example. Before I became a dad, I would never have imagined that a human being could pee on their own head. Now I know. Such is the wisdom we learn.

By the power vested in me by my dozen years' experience as a priest, my forty-plus years as a Christian, and the piece of paper certifying me as a master of divinity, I tell you that the best way to learn about this Jesus thing is to play with it. Try it on. Imagine yourself in the stories of the Bible. Imagine alternate endings. Write psalms and poetry. Preach to the birds in your backyard. Let God's gift of play teach you about its giver.

For one whole year I prayed the same thing every day, and each of those 365 days I received in my mind the very same response verbatim. Every day I prayed, "God teach me to be holy. Teach me to be close to you." I felt a wash of peace and these simple words came to my mind: "Les, every step is holy."

It has been said that beginning improvisers are trying to figure out what will happen, and advanced improvisers realize that it already has. The human soul's natural state is to be alive in the moment, playing with the God of creation, and discovering the depth of our redemption, but that doesn't fit in our plans or strategies. At about day 295 of asking that same question in prayer and getting the same answer, I began to wonder if I was dumb. While the answer to that musing is probably yes, I don't think that's why I needed it repeated so often for so long. This insight that every moment is an invitation to grow closer is inconceivably beautiful. We are graced with the precious opportunity to show our love for the Source of Love in every moment.

In Genesis 2 God made the first human being, but he was lonely, so God made each of the animals. But God let that human give each animal their name. What a wonderful game—to play the world into existence. How wonderful that God would create the whole wild universe just to help fill the hole in God's new friend's heart. Not just that God did it *for* that first human, but that God had the tenacity and patience to do it *with* him. In divine wisdom, God decided to empower us, to put us on stage, so to speak, as we work out our salvation together. **Shakespeare was right. "All the world's a stage," but God never gave us a script. I assume that is because we are expected to improvise.**

The Toy Airplane and the Holy Eucharist

Not only is play a great teacher, it may be the only thing qualified to demonstrate the kind of love, grace, and forgiveness that we are talking about when we talk about Jesus.

There is this boy in my congregation. When he was little and he would come up for communion with his family, you could tell his attention was pulled in all directions. Sitting still is not easy for most boys. Kneeling still at the altar rail is nearly impossible for some. His mother was so sweet and so respectful. Being a parent myself, I understood the difficulty of trying to corral your kid in public. This boy was particularly interesting, though, because he always had a toy airplane in his hand. My guess was the object soothed him. Pretty soon he wanted to share his game with me. When I came up to him with the bread in my hand, he would move the toy through the air like it was flying and make a big "zooooooom" noise.

Many priests would have discouraged this behavior, but my heart is playful and my mind is trained in "Yes, &." Without even thinking I joined the game. I took the wafer (the consecrated host) and flew it myself, making the exact same "zooooooom" noise and landing it in his hand.

I had shared this special ritual with the kid for months, and then one Sunday I noticed his mom. Like I said, she was so sweet and respectful and genuinely appreciative of my ministry, and I realized just how hard she was working to corral her son. I began to wonder, "Am I making a mistake by playing with him at the rail?" His mother was trying to teach him how to behave in public; I was probably making that job harder.

I thought about it a lot, and I decided to keep the game going. His mother had an important job. She had to teach him how to succeed in the world, but I had a different job. My job as a priest was to teach this kid what the abundant grace of God is like. Her job was important and hard. So was mine—and even though we approached the boy from different sides of the rail, something makes me think that the balance was important.

I don't know of anything as useful in teaching God's character as a highly skilled aptitude for playfulness. Yet playful is an adjective that few would use to describe their church community. But if play is such an important teacher, why do we lock it up when things get serious? Often people talk about the importance of humor in facing tough situations. Doubtless you have heard the old cliché, "You have to laugh, or you will just cry." I have always found that expression odd. One, I have no problem with crying, and, two, it makes humor seem like it is just for pressure relief. It is so much more than that. A sense of playfulness is delicate. It can be easily stifled, but if it is nourished, it can change the fabric and feel of a community. It will also multiply the community's adaptive qualities and grow a sense of identity and connection. As I like to say, **a joke is a gift of amusement, but laughter is an invitation into deeper relationship**.

Discussion Questions and Brain Exercise

Since the idea of using playfulness as a measure of church is new for many folks, I recommend some reflection. Take some time to think about the level of playfulness in your life and church. It is a surprisingly useful thing to assess. Hopefully going through the questions below will leave you with both gratitude and insight.

1. List your favorite activities outside of church.
2. List your favorite activities in church.
3. On a scale of one to five, how playful are each of those activities?
4. How playful is your community of faith (however you define it)?
5. How playful is your worship time?
6. What can you think of that you could do to make that time more playful? •

Playfulness Helps You See Outside Yourself

Early in my ministry the Episcopal Church was wrapped in a debate over who should be invited to take communion. It appears to be settled now, at least in the sense that people aren't really arguing about it that much anymore. It is the tradition and rule of the Episcopal Church that all baptized people are invited to take communion. Until 1979, you had to be a confirmed Episcopalian to receive communion, and many believed that opening it up to all baptized people was a radical step toward inclusion. But by the time I started getting more involved in church, people had begun to wonder whether we had gone far enough. Many clergy began saying that all those who desire a deeper connection with Jesus should be welcome.

If communion isn't your thing, this debate may seem ridiculous, and maybe it is, but Episcopalians as a whole tend to be *really* into communion. It is why we call our clergy "priests."[1]

I always was and still am on the side of the more inclusive approach, which did not win the day. While I get the arguments that the early church made people go through intensive processes of education and commitment and ultimately baptism before they could receive communion, and I understand we usually look to the Last Supper as the foundation for communion (and that was held in the upper room with the most dedicated and committed people Jesus knew), I have counterarguments. But I'm not bringing all this up to relitigate the question. I want to show how play can change your perspective.

I was newly out of seminary and, as I said, this topic was hot. I had written papers on it. And made up talking points. Then one day I went for a prayer walk. I decided to look at the wonders of nature and listen to cheesy pop music. I stopped just thinking about the issue and started playfully praying about it. Before I knew it, a whole parable fell into my head as if I had tripped over the whole thing. It didn't come word by word, but all at once. While I don't think it is actually about the communion question, it did give me clarity about why the issue was bothering me so much and, more importantly, it showed me how to have peace with my limited role as a clergyperson trying to teach about the incomprehensible grace of God. Here is what

---

1. Technically a "priest" is someone who performs a sacrifice, such as killing an animal on an altar. Christian traditions with a strong view of Holy Communion will use the term "priest" because we see the sacrament as spiritually connected to Christ's sacrifice on the cross. I always have to be careful, though. When people find out I am a priest who is married with kids, the Catholic baggage confuses them, but the term "priest" has to do with Eucharistic theology, not with whether or not you can have a hot date.

came to me as I was skipping along the riverbanks of Broad Ripple in Indianapolis.

The Parable of the Plate

Once upon a time, in a diocese far, far away, there was a deeply obedient old priest who served in a Benedictine monastery and retreat center. One Wednesday, as the monks were having their daily Mass, a Stranger walked in the back of the chapel. The brothers were accustomed to having visitors, but only on the weekends. The midweek services were only the faithful few.

The old priest couldn't help but notice the Stranger was fumbling through the worship books in the back of the church, clearly unable to keep up. When it came time for communion, all the pious monks gathered in a circle around the altar to receive. Once they had, the old priest realized that the Stranger was still sitting in the back. Not wanting to exclude the poor soul, the priest took the paten (the plate of communion bread) and walked to the back of the chapel to offer the Stranger communion.

When he arrived, the Stranger whispered, "No, Father. I am sorry. I can't."

The old priest was surprised. "Why not?"

"Well," said the Stranger, "I have studied Christianity and I know that you have a rule. Only baptized people can receive communion. I am not baptized. Father, I am a stranger to your people."

The old priest felt stuck for a moment. He was not the type to break a rule on a whim, but he did not want to exclude the Stranger. For a moment, he stood there nodding. Then he said, "What you have said is true, and there is another rule as well."

"What is that?" asked the Stranger.

"Our rule of life clearly states that we are to treat the stranger as if he is Christ Himself. So, would you do me the honor of serving me?" And he handed the Stranger the plate.

Notes on the Parable

Don't get me wrong. I don't think this is a realistic thing to do with a church visitor; it would either seem too strange or too intimate. But the Benedictine strategy of seeing the stranger as Christ is an important part of fostering an authentic Christian community. The old priest in the story pulls a classic "Yes, &," both saying "yes" to the rules and adding the larger message of curious faithfulness. Improv teaches us to treat our partners as if they were geniuses. Christian faith teaches us to treat the stranger as Christ himself.

See how different things can look? Ten minutes of play did more for me than years of study.

Chapter 8

Un-leadership

Specialized versus Collaborative Teamwork

When improv works, it seems magical. One of the main reasons is because improv uses a different kind of teamwork than most of us are used to. Teamwork is a huge part of organizational leadership. While I am sure that you could cut teamwork into more and more categories, for the purpose of this book I am going to talk about two different kinds of teamwork: specialized and collaborative.

Specialized teamwork is by far the most common. It can be simple or quite complex. In its most simple form, specialized teamwork is about dividing tasks among people to increase efficiency. You wash the dishes, and I will dry. Even though you are specialized, the team still has to coordinate. The dryer can only dry as fast as the washer washes, which means that there may be downtime for the dryer that could also be used to put the dishes away. The washer will also by definition be done first, so they can take a longer break afterward because they had the more intense job.[1]

---

1. If this seems like a long conversation on washing dishes, it is because the power went out for a day while I was writing this book, so I had a lot of time at the sink next to my wife to think about it.

As tasks become more complex, specialization requires increased communication and a heightened organizational structure. Hierarchies develop and schedules are made to make sure that all the different jobs are done in ways that fit together. Those hierarchies also become responsible for solving conflicts that arise from the specialization. Those who hinder the progress of the organization are replaced. In short, management develops.

One of the real drawbacks of specialized teamwork (especially in a larger organization) is that the creativity of how to approach problem-solving and how to structure the organization most efficiently tends to narrow to only a few top executives. Only so many brains work on improving the "how" of the organization.

Business leaders have come up with some interesting models to maximize the efficiency of specialized teamwork and to decentralize creativity in the organization. For example, *The 4 Disciplines of Execution*[2] (which isn't anywhere near as scary as it sounds) recommends that an organization have one focus area and then create a game-like structure so the employees are invested in finding more efficient ways of meeting their goals themselves. For example, an organization of valets wanted to decrease wait time for cars. They put the data up on a board for workers of every level to see. One of the valets thought, "If I give my customers a slip with the phone number of the booth, they can call down ahead of time and I will get them out quicker." Before you knew it, not only had that firm changed, so had the entire organization. There are extreme benefits to allowing creativity to come from every level of an organization if the ideas can be managed. One of the things *The 4 Disciplines* does well is force the top of the organization to be clear about what

---

2. Chris McChesney, Sean Covey, and Jim Huling, *The 4 Disciplines of Execution: Achieving Your Wildly Important Goals* (New York: Free Press, 2016).

they care about, which empowers the other parts of the company to focus on the "how."

Collaborative teamwork, however, is categorically different. Many of the strategies that make specialized teamwork effective get in the way of collaboration. Collaborative teamwork is putting your heads together on something. When creativity can be done in concert, it becomes more than the sum of its parts. When a team knows how to work collaboratively, they discover brilliant, beautiful, and hilarious ideas that no one person could do on their own. All of improv is focused on creating real-time collaborative teamwork.[3]

If this seems strange, think about the most basic directions a team is given when they are working on a problem together rather than managing a group of independent tasks. We are told to "brainstorm," to come up with a series of ideas and not to evaluate them until we are done. We start by focusing on getting out all the ideas we can come up with. It is cliché, but as someone who leads meetings for a living, let me tell you it is effective. Even though we all know that it is the best way to operate, I don't think I have ever been in a brainstorming session where I didn't have to remind the group at least three times to hold off on the evaluation. There may be some deep-seated psychological reason for all this, or it may be simpler than that. The critical voice (of both self and others) is esteemed in specialized teamwork, but it is the death blow to collaboration. The analytical one in specialized teamwork is the boss—the one with the most status. That is who everyone wants to be, because everyone has been trained by the ubiquity of specialized teamwork. Remember the "Yes and No" exercise. "No" brings control, but "yes" brings power.

---

3. Or team*play*, if you prefer.

How Traits Work in the Different Types of Teamwork

Trait	Specialized	Collaborative
Analytical thinking	Highly valued.	Limits effectiveness during the creative time.
Hierarchy	Invaluable to make sure tasks are clear and created on time.	Counterproductive. Status will add or subtract weight from ideas without regard for the idea's actual value.
Quality control	Invaluable. Everything must be held to a standard of uniform quality.	Counterproductive. No good idea is ever found without going through at least ten bad ones.
Competitiveness	Fantastic. Makes the team self-manage.	Terrible. The individual wants to hold up his partners, not one-up them.
Playfulness	Distraction.	The ground of trust and the source of the creative spark.
Positive attitude	Great if you are a subordinate. Unnecessary and unexpected if you are management.	A MUST for anyone in power.
Trust	Comes from accountability.	Comes from mutual goals.
Sense of mystery about what the final project will look like	Disastrous. What happens if the pieces don't fit?	Necessity. It is needed to distribute creativity throughout the organization.

Ad Agency

I first realized how fundamentally different the demands of collaborative leadership are while playing one of the most introductory games known in the improv world. I had an advantage that night over my classmates. I had taken the class before. I like to tell people that I took level one twice because I flunked the first time. Actually, there were not enough people to make a level two class, so they let me retake level one for free while they gathered more students. For this reason, I remembered the game of "Ad Agency." The game is more for practice than performance. It is done to get people used to how it feels when you can trust that every idea you have will be met with enthusiasm and support.

It goes like this: a small group of four or five improvisers are told that they work at an ad agency, and that they are going to have to plan an entire ad campaign around a product. The product is usually something wacky they get by putting together different suggestions from the audience: a "hairy automobile" or a "stinky soda." One of the improvisers is told that they are the boss, the "ad exec," and that they have one job—to meet every idea with ridiculous enthusiasm. You can bet that the campaign won't make coherent sense, but it's quite entertaining to see the players scramble to come up with something, and they always do.

That night, though, the first group didn't get all the directions for the game. A competent young woman was told that she was the boss. The actor was a college professor, and clearly was used to the kind of leadership and teamwork we see all the time in the working world. But our improv teacher didn't give her the direction to be enthusiastic. I don't know if that was a mistake or intentional, but what happened was so interesting.

Like I said, I remembered the exercise from the first time I took level one. I knew it was supposed to be about going with the ideas wherever they took you. But the woman playing the ad exec didn't know that. So, she ran a normal meeting. She was nice and cordial, positive even, but she evaluated every idea. She was truly playing an executive (though a relatively good one). One member of the team saw the exercise as a game rather than a task. She made wild suggestions that the exec shut down. I noticed that the more times the one with the ideas was told "No," the wilder and more unrealistic the suggestions became until she just stopped participating. By the end of the scene, they had come up with an ad campaign that was not bad. Our teacher then pointed out that what the wild suggester said was not incorporated into the project even once as they moved forward. He also pointed out that the audience laughed every time the wild suggester talked and didn't laugh once at the exec.

I don't tell this story to give the exec a hard time, in fact quite the opposite. It was the second session and she jumped into the middle of it all; as I said, she was kind and polite and committed to keeping the group on task. She was leading well by every standard I had seen before I walked into an improv theater, yet what she did utterly failed. And I learned something watching her. **Collaborative leadership abhors hierarchy.**

The Downward Cycle of Disempowerment

Did you notice how I said that the wild suggester got wilder and more unrealistic the more she was told "no"? I find this is true in organizations too. When groups of people or committees are told "no" to their ideas and the leadership does what it was going to do anyway, that erodes trust. What is also interesting is that when people don't think their ideas are being heard, they start to make worse and worse suggestions. I have seen this over and over with church committees. I once went to a stewardship committee with the idea of having people meet in homes to discuss the pledges—what is often called an "every member canvass." As soon as I talked about it, I felt the energy drop like a lead balloon. Apparently, the former priest had pushed a similar program and it had left a sour taste in people's mouths. We kept talking and someone suggested we send handwritten notes inviting parishioners to a fellowship event at the church. Was that the stewardship committee's job? No. Did it avoid the topic of money when that was exactly what the stewardship committee was supposed to be talking about? Absolutely. I said, "Okay, we will start working on the notes," and we did.

The next meeting, someone asked about the "cottage meetings" in homes.

I said, "You all said 'no' to that. You thought it was a bad idea." The room looked dumbfounded.

"Oh," said the guy who asked. "Well, I thought you were going to have us do it anyway."

I responded, "No, we work on this together."

A couple years later that same committee came up with some of the most fun, powerful, and wonderful stuff I had ever seen in a church stewardship drive. You can find some examples on St. Aidan's (Cypress, Texas) YouTube channel. But be prepared to see my greatest spiritual gift, which is my willingness to look like an idiot. This along with some other poignant experiences led me to one of my axioms for ministry: **If you don't take the lay volunteer's work seriously, neither will they; it will decrease their creativity and their suggestions will seem progressively dumber. The group will also become more vocal until the leader finally pays attention.**

The Upward Cycle of Empowerment

Straight out of seminary I was called to do young adult ministry (ages twenty-one to thirty-five) at a church in the Midwest. They wanted to start a Sunday evening service primarily to attract more young adults. A dream job. I got paid to hang out with a bunch of people my age, and talk about Jesus, and I got to design a completely new worship experience. For the church, it made sense not just from a missional perspective but from a demographical one as well. The church was surrounded by a relatively funky area of town with a retail strip nestled in a neighborhood of small homes that seemed to alternate between retired couples that owned their home and couples in their twenties who rented.

Planting a new worship service was hard work, and it was a lot of fun. One of the most interesting things was going through each piece of our worship with a group of young adults and discussing what was meaningful and what could be let go.

Going through the service chunk by chunk, we eventually got to the section where most of my anxiety lives. I asked them what they were looking for out of the sermon. Preaching is a remarkably personal and vulnerable act. It is hard to give or receive meaningful feedback because, by definition, the preacher is talking about the things that matter most to them. However, I knew it was important, so I hoped that the feedback wouldn't hurt too much.

I took a deep breath and asked, "What are you looking for out of a sermon?"

The first comment came immediately. No awkward pause. "A conversation."

Mystified, I looked around the room. Everyone was nodding. It was the most surprising consensus I had ever seen, and I can read a room pretty well. It was also more than a little scary for me because I took actual preaching classes, but no one ever taught me how to preach as a conversation. I took the feedback and over the next three years or so I preached like that almost every week. It was one of the most interesting and rewarding experiences I have had as a priest.[4]

The most profound thing I learned about conversational preaching was how incredibly insightful laypeople can be if they are given a supportive environment. If you lead conversational sermons in a way that is affirming, not only will you grow as a conversation leader, the congregation will also grow as a preacher. Don't get me wrong. It doesn't start strong. It starts like an awkward seedling and grows into an oak. In the beginning, my conversational sermons were clunky and had some profoundly awkward moments. Every so often,

---

4. See the appendix to find out more about preaching a conversational sermon.

someone would make an extreme political statement assuming everyone was in agreement. I learned to say something like, "So that is really important to you . . ." and summarize their point, so I could both validate the individual and individuate their opinion, making it safe for others to disagree.

More often, people came up with things that seemed completely irrelevant. I didn't understand it at the time, but my improv training was helping me connect the dots back to the scripture of the day and the topic of the conversation. For a while in the first year, some of the regulars said that they came just to see how I would handle the curveballs. Still, bringing the topics back around and panning for the gold of what the congregants had to say was exhilarating for both me and them. I still think they should make a Mountain Dew ad about X-Treme preaching.

At first, it felt like most of the random stuff came from the same two or three people, but what I found after two or three months was that those people began to get used to the idea that I actually paid attention to what they had to say. If it was rough, or they couldn't find the words, I would help them and they began to talk a lot less, or what they said was more relevant and often meaningful.

Soon the conversations started to have their own ebb and flow. Our small gathering of thirty to fifty began to reveal something to me about faith. For the first time in my life, I recognized what a grace-filled community was. Not only were individuals finding their faith and learning to articulate it, the community as a whole was transforming spiritually as well.

I didn't think about it at the time, but the conversational sermon was "Yes, &." I would prep with all these things to say and put them in my back pocket. I found that if I said much on the front end of the sermon, the conversation would fall flat because the authority had spoken. Without my realizing it, that authority stifled the more honest, more vulnerable questions. By the end of my time there, I opened every sermon by saying something like, "What pops out at you?"

That made it easy for people to share the interesting, challenging, or strange. Then I was in the perfect position to say, "Yes," and I could connect it to one of my back pocket thoughts.

Preaching there was exciting, because no matter how much I thought I had exhausted a topic, someone would chime in with something I had never thought or heard before. Once we were talking about how Jesus taught forgiveness, but there was a point where even Jesus said, "Let go and treat the person as a Gentile to you." One man popped up and said, "And how are we supposed to treat Gentiles according to Jesus? LOVE them." With so many different perspectives swirling around, we soon realized that God was revealing God's self through our many voices, usually in harmony, sometimes in dissonance, but always in rhythm. The sermon was no longer something I preached; it became something we experienced.

This young adult service sparked a profound intergenerational connection and community. When I first asked the focus group what they wanted, they talked about connections to older adults. I wasn't sure about that initially, because of some of my own baggage. I didn't really trust people over forty to be supportive of those in their twenties and thirties. But the conversational sermon showed me how right the focus group was.

Every so often a big event pulled either the younger or the older crowd away for one evening. A football game would kill my younger group; bad weather or the prospect of driving in the dark would keep away the older folks. Whenever that happened, the conversational sermon would lose much of its magic. When it was just the older folks, the conversation fell into clichés and it was difficult to get people to engage the unpleasant side of the text. When it was just the young adults, the attention tended to wander and the conversation went in circles.

Before I was ordained, I attended a church plant for a couple years: the Church of the Advocate in Chapel Hill, North Carolina. The vicar, the Rev. Lisa G. Fischbeck, began every service by saying that the word "liturgy" (an alternate word for worship) literally means the work of the people, and that we believed that worship is different because of each person there. Little did I know that after my ordination I would see such a clear example and expression of that vision as my congregation huddled together, shared the best of our insights, and celebrated the Eucharist using the baptismal font as an altar.[5]

It was the miracle that made way for the process. What I didn't understand at the time was that collaboration was the key to forming disciples and Christian community. We all need a place that accepts us for who we are and encourages us into who we are becoming. A conversational sermon isn't the only means to that goal, but it made obvious what had always been true. That is how the original disciples learned. They were with Jesus day in and day out. They touched the hands that reached out to the leper. They shared meals with the one who multiplied loaves and fishes. They learned grace in their ragtag floating commune as their teacher hung in with them despite their consistent failure to understand what he was talking about. **A supportive, loving community making their theology together in real time can form a true disciple, and in fact it is probably the only thing that ever has.**

---

5. This was another happy accident. When we were first organizing the service, we really liked the idea of it meeting people in the back of the church. There was this beautiful, rounded area (it had been the apse before they renovated the area and moved the altar to the far side of the space), and we really enjoyed the vision of meeting people who could barely make their way into this church, which was both beautiful and intimidating. We also wanted to fit one hundred chairs in there, which we could comfortably, but then there would be no room for the altar. Such a blessing, that challenge. There was this fantastic marble baptismal font that was huge. We got a custom-cut plexiglass top so that we could both have room for the chairs and combine the beauty of the two great sacraments by blessing Holy Communion directly above the waters of baptism.

Back to the Point and to the Ad Agency

The practices of improv create a space where the community as a whole can be in charge. That doesn't mean that there aren't status differences between players, or that a collaborative group might exist within a hierarchical structure. The conversational sermon gave me a ministry application of what I was learning in improv. There are ways to have a functional community and take everyone seriously. When we have a community that values each person, every person gets to participate in deep and meaningful ways. I began to wonder how those other improv lessons might be consistent with the church I was called to serve.

I began thinking about what I knew about church leadership. Since 1979 and the current edition of the Book of Common Prayer, the Episcopal Church became increasingly focused on the ministry of the laypeople, but while the church has spent a lot of time reenvisioning the role of the laity, we haven't always done as much work on redefining the priesthood itself.

I remember when I was in the ordination process in the late 90s and early 2000s. I can't count the number of times I was invited to talk about the importance of lay ministry, and how wonderful that ministry was—which is great. But I don't recall one time where I was asked about how I saw my role as a priest in that process—and I was a layperson applying to be a priest. I am fervently pro-lay leadership, but in a church that is all about lay empowerment, what does it mean to be a priest?

Then I remembered what happened when I watched the second group in the improv class try Ad Agency. The teacher made it clear this time that the exec was supposed to love literally everything. It didn't make for a great ad campaign by professional standards, but it was so fun. The crazy ideas kept coming, and coming together. People built off each other. They did naturally what the first group had forced. The different players began to move together with the ideas as the intensity grew, and they ended the scene by improvising a song together that was the jingle for the fake and ridiculous product.

Watching it happen took the breath from my lungs. I witnessed a community of strangers working *together* with real collaboration and no defined leader. Instead of the hierarchy the world assumes necessary, these random people in their second improv class trusted the creative spirit to shelter and lead them. And it worked. I remember thinking, "Wow. I have been a Christian my entire life. I have preached on servant leadership countless times. And this is the first time I have really seen it in action." That exercise seemed truer to acting the way Christians believe than anything I had ever seen in a vestry meeting.

"What would happen," I thought to myself, "if we ran churches with this kind of supportive chaos? It would probably be nuts and unruly, but at least it would be fun."

Exercise: Ad Agency

Gather some church friends and play Ad Agency. It can't hurt. I hate to break it to you, but your game nights were already kinda boring.

1. Get a group together of four to six people. Find a volunteer to be the executive. Tell them they are going to be putting together an ad campaign and that the executive's job is to love everything that is said.
2. Get a suggestion for the product to advertise. It can literally be anything. Usually it is good to have one person give the noun and another an adjective. That helps with a wacky final product.
3. Then tell them to go! Call scene when you get a big laugh.
4. Make sure you get several groups to play several times. After each scene ask the people what their favorite moments were, and ask the players to talk about what it was like to make stuff up when they knew the exec would love it. •

Status and Grace-Filled Leadership

The Ad Agency game is so powerful because of the marriage of positivity and status. The positivity is powerful on its own, but the fact that it comes from the executive, the one in charge, is what makes the game ridiculously lovely. It also makes it seem novel since we unconsciously assume the role of the leader is to say "no." Understanding how status works and its pitfalls is crucial to making a collaborative team on the stage or in the chancel. If ignored, status differences can destroy any hope of true collaboration in a community.

Status is an extremely important concept for understanding human relationships. Our relationship with relative status is so ingrained that it feels like instinct. Understanding those relationships and how to poke at them is a useful way to approach an improv scene. One very common exercise in improv classes is to put a card from a deck of playing cards on each student's head, with the card facing out. People can see everyone else's card but not their own. They are told that the card represents their status. The ace is the CEO and the two is the janitor. Then people play as if they are at a party. After about five minutes of interaction, you ask the group to line up from low status to high. I have seen this played many times. While the group never gets the order perfect, they end up ridiculously close to guessing the actual pecking order. That shouldn't be surprising. We know how to negotiate status. We do it every day.

Once improvisers get the drift of this social game, they have a lot of fun with it. We are used to people staying in their lane and occasionally fighting for higher status, but try playing a scene where two actors are competing to see whose character can have the lowest status.

Actor 1: After you.
Actor 2: No, I couldn't, after you.

It is hilarious.

In his book on improv and Christian ethics, Sam Wells points out that high and low status are just different strategies of trying to get what you want. You can be commanding or complementary. We are trained by the world to think of high status as preferable, but it is often the lower-status one who actually wins. If there is an argument and you want it to end, you say, "No, really. I feel terrible. I am so sorry," which makes it difficult for the other person to keep the fight going. As Wells points out, "I am sorry" can be the most manipulative phrase in the English language.

We can't look at Christ naked and beaten on the cross and think that status was what he was after. Jesus was what Wells calls a "master player." Because status was not linked to worth in his mind, Jesus could use high-status plays when they were useful, like driving the money changers out of the temple, and low-status gestures when they were useful, like washing the disciples' feet.[6]

However, despite all our "servant leadership" language, the church has definite status relationships, and based on the outfits in the Episcopal Church, they are laughingly obvious. I tend to prefer lower-status strategies like self-deprecating humor or naming what I admire in the people around me, but when they were teaching high status in an improv class I was taking, I was surprised by something. They explained that when you play high status it is not only good to keep straight posture in your back, but you also don't want to move or tilt your neck much. I got into the physical stance they described and I remember thinking, "Wow, this is familiar." Then I realized the clerical collar literally keeps your head in the high-status position; everything I was doing with my body reminded me of having vestments on.

---

6. Samuel Wells, *Improvisation: The Drama of Christian Ethics* (Grand Rapids, MI: Brazos Press, 2004), 87–104.

I am not suggesting that as Christians we completely reject the notion of status. It is too ingrained in our world. That would be like trying to run a marathon while holding our breath. But if our Lord washed the disciples' feet and told them that they should wash each other's feet,[7] then we should probably take seriously the ways that we can take status from the powerful and give it freely and without reservation.

---

7. John 13:1–17. By the way, if you read that section of the Gospel of John, it is a master class in using both high and low status. Jesus is commanding them as their rabbi to receive his service. And he is literally doing the job of a slave. So he goes high, only to pivot to low. Then he tells his disciples that because he is their master, they aren't better then him—taking high status again. And so they also should wash each other's feet (i.e., take low status). To borrow an analogy from Wells, the status moves up and down like a seesaw.

Chapter 9

Un-leadership and the Church of Pentecost

Church and Pentecost

In the last chapter, I said that the shared leadership of the second Ad Agency game seemed truer to Christian beliefs than the way churches are generally run. I say that because of one story in the Bible. It is the account of the Church's birth: the story of Pentecost.

I love the Bible with all my heart. However, one of my deepest frustrations with teaching the Bible is that people put it on a pedestal. We tell each other in both unconscious and direct ways that it is special and holy and deserves reverence, so we put it on a different plane of existence. But here is my thing: I don't think the Bible exists to live on a pedestal and gather dust. I mean, have you read it? Soap operas got nothing on this book full of sex, violence, stupidity, and mysterious contradiction. I think we put the Bible on a pedestal too quickly. It isn't an object to be admired; it is a ladder to climb. So much of it is written as a story to be read *as a story*. In my enthusiasm to bring people into the actual Bible stories, sometimes I come across as irreverent. Please know that I am not trying to make fun of the Bible. I am trying to reveal the humor that I believe is rightfully there. Remember, too, the church took decades to write these stories down. In the beginning of the faith, the church preferred firsthand storytelling to a written account. To me this indicates that an essential part of the tradition is not just its text, but also playing with its delivery. With that in mind, I present Pentecost: crazy, incredible, miraculous, and ridiculous.

Crazy

The book of Acts is clearly a sequel. The first paragraph is addressed to the same person as the beginning of the Gospel of Luke, and the author is talking about it being his second book—the second volume of Luke's two-part series on the church's story. It starts with Jesus's resurrection and then in the first paragraph describes Jesus floating up to heaven, leaving some bizarre instructions about how the disciples should wait around for the Holy Spirit (1:4–5).

The disciples said, "Wait!" That is not what they were expecting. They had their hopes hung on Jesus being a kick-butt military leader who was supposed to liberate his people from Roman rule. They asked Jesus if he was going to actually fix stuff before he left. Jesus gave kind of a cagey answer about how it wasn't for them to know when stuff was going to be fixed, but to wait there in Jerusalem; the Holy Spirit would come and they would be sent all over the world (1:1–8).

The disciples (apostles maybe? *apostlesish?*) waited. They realized that they were a man down because of Judas, so they cast lots (the ancient equivalent of flipping a coin) to see who got his spot. Think about this for a second. These eleven who had walked with Jesus and were the ones he was counting on filled a vacancy with a quick game of gambling because they had nothing to do other than wait. Not only that, it was a gamble between two guys: Matthias, who won, and the other guy who has three aliases: Joseph, Barsabbas, and Justus (1:12–26). A guy who we literally never hear about again.

If you know your Hebrew Bible, there are some connections to be made about the fact that Jesus ascended forty days after his resurrection and the Holy Spirit came on the fiftieth, but Luke's audience was not primarily Jewish and had no idea about these things. Luke doesn't take the time to explain. Such is the opening to the book of Acts. Things are crazy—and the first thing is a command to hang out for ten days.

Incredible

The story goes from crazy to something that seems more fit for a fantasy novel. There is a rush of wind to build suspense, and then a swarm of burning tongues. Not heads or mouths, just tongues and they are on fire. The tongues split up and rested on each of the disciples (apostles? *Disposals?*). All of them were filled with the Holy Spirit and they began to speak in other languages (2:1–4).

This "filled with the Holy Spirit thing" is a big deal. The Holy Spirit was (and is) the presence of God. The Holy Spirit exists in the Bible and filled prophets and leaders. The presence of the Spirit is special, rare, and marks a turning point.

Miraculous

The gift the Spirit gave them was to speak in other languages. Many Bibles translate this as "tongues," which is a good literal translation and lines up well with the "tongues of fire." By the way, the "sound like the rush of a violent wind" also lined up with the coming of the Holy Spirit, because the Greek word for "spirit" can also be translated as "wind"—a biblical pun—or at least a double entendre in the very birth of the church. But I point the "tongues" thing out because it is often misunderstood.

As the disciples spoke, the diverse group of people present each heard the words in their own native language. The miracle was one of understanding and communication.

The Hebrew Bible holds the story of the tower of Babel, where people banded together to build something great for themselves. They wanted to appear God-like. Their plan was thwarted, however, when God stepped in and separated their languages and made it so that they couldn't work together to try to appear to be what they were not. That story is redeemed at Pentecost with a beautiful "Yes, &."

At Pentecost, the apostles banded together, but not to make something for themselves. They worked together with the Spirit's mystifying presence to build the church. One detail I love about this story is that it was not that God just made them all speak the same language; God made everyone *hear* in their unique and diverse languages. That is why it is a "Yes, &." Yes, people are selfish and that has led to different languages, and when it comes to the church, that selfishness will not stand in the way of the work of the Spirit. The ending doesn't undo the middle; it completes the story by bringing both the beginning and the end into one justified resolution.[1]

What is also a beautiful "&" about this miracle is that this was not what the apostles were looking for. Remember their question to Jesus before he left. It wasn't "When are we going to meet God and save these hungry souls of foreigners by uniting all people in God's kingdom?" That was what Jesus had been talking about, but it wasn't what the the disciples heard. They wanted to restore Israel—their nation. **What a hilariously, frustratingly fantastic miracle that the first gift to the newborn church is the supernatural ability to talk to people they don't care about.**

---

1. When I say "justified," I mean in the technical improv sense of justification. Remember in improv, justification is taking the tension of two things that don't fit and making a path for them to fit. Remember the A, C, what's the B? exercise. A is different languages, C is the church working together, and the B is the miraculous diversity of understanding.

I am laughing out loud right now. I told you I love the Bible.

The Acts of the Apostles is really the chronicles of the Holy Spirit and the pathetic sidekicks trying to keep up. Once you get that, the whole book becomes hilarious, ironic, and beautiful. Even the mis-naming becomes funny because it just reinforces the theological slapstick of the book itself.

Ridiculous

On the other hand, if you still haven't seen the humor in the story yet, something is about to happen which is undeniably funny. Luke wove this picture of what looks like the most amazing experience of all time, leaving the reader to wonder what it must have been like to be a part of such an awe-inspiring moment. Then Luke tells us that some guys saw it and said, "Those fools are just drunk" (Acts 2:13).

What a cold blanket on the whole story.

"Actually," Peter retorted, "I know you think these people are drunk, but they aren't. They can't be; it is only nine in the morning!"

The Bible literally says that in Acts 2:15. Every year we read this story in church and every year I audibly laugh at that line. But it does more than reveal that Peter was not the kind of guy you invite to the good parties; it shows how the miracle of the presence of God over-took some and was seen as ridiculous and forgettable by others.

This birth story of the church makes it clear lots of people are not going to get it. They can't or won't experience the miracle that is right in front of them. It bakes doubt into the system from the very beginning.

Pentecost's Implication for Church Leadership

So Peter had the floor and the challenge of explaining to the skeptical crowd what is happening. He quoted from the Hebrew Bible and the book of Joel:

In the last days it will be, God declares,
that I will pour out my Spirit upon all flesh,
   and your sons and your daughters shall prophesy,
and your young men shall see visions,
   and your old men shall dream dreams.
Even upon my slaves, both men and women,
   in those days I will pour out my Spirit;
      and they shall prophesy. (Acts 2:17–18)

Remember the role that the Holy Spirit, the very presence of God, has played in the Bible up until this point. The Holy Spirit anointed the prophets. Her[2] presence was rare and only the most chosen heard the word and guidance. But here is an alternative vision of the way that God interacts with God's people. This passage is full of reversals. Wisdom is usually thought of as coming with age, but in this passage the prophecy comes from the young. Similarly, dreaming of the future and imagining what is possible is usually thought of as the fancy of the young, but it is the old people that will dream dreams. "Even upon my slaves, both men and women, in those days I will pour out my Spirit." No one is exempt or unqualified to have the word of God spoken through them. Throughout the Hebrew Bible, God picked prophets from outside of the establishment. Amos, for example, was an outsider. God also picked insiders like Isaiah. The work of the Holy Spirit has always been wily and unpredictable, and it was all over this new community.

---

2. I say "her" because in both Greek and Hebrew the word for "spirit" is a feminine word. Both of those languages assign gender to all kinds of things which contemporary English does not. Some would call the Spirit an "it." However, translating the Spirit of God as an "it" seems to diminish her dynamic quality and undercuts my approach to Acts, which assumes the Holy Spirit herself to be a foundational (though mystical) character.

Come Pentecost, God was not an absentee landlord any longer. The church of Acts is not a game of follow the leader; it is a game of follow the Spirit.

How would you structure a community where you believe that God is truly active and speaking from anyone, anywhere, at any time? Would it look like a board meeting, or would it look like the Ad Agency game?

You can tell my answer to that question. That is not to say that there don't need to be systems of accountability or people in authority to discern what is from God and what wolves are trying to sneak their way in. But if we really believe that God is everywhere and can and does lead and speak through anyone, then Christian leaders need to have an instinct to say "yes" and work together in real time with what the Spirit is doing.

Chapter 10

Practical Methods for Changing Culture and Worldview

So far, I've made arguments for why collaborative leadership is truer to our theological understanding of the church and why "Yes, &" is the best model for a graceful reflection of God from the Beloved Community. Now I want to make a very practical appeal. **Collaborative "Yes, &" leadership is the only thing I know which can dependably change the culture of an organization.**

This tool is as necessary to a church leader as a wrench is to a plumber. I don't want to brag, but changing organizational culture is where I excel as a priest. It is not bragging because I learned how to do it completely by accident.

When I was just a couple years out of seminary, a diocesan canon asked me to lead a workshop for clergy on how to make managed change in a congregation. I laughed out loud. I was a wimpy assistant and the group she was referring me to had clergy with over ten years' experience. At the time, I had started a new evening service at my church that was getting some traction and she told me that I actually had more experience with managing change than many of my colleagues with greater tenure.

I still don't think I am an expert, but looking back on my career, it is something that I know how to do. I have already shared a little about how in my first call as a priest, I was hired to do young adult ministry. There wasn't much of a skeleton for such a program in the congregation and almost no working model in the Episcopal Church. While the church was supportive in theory, when I arrived it became clear that the church culture wasn't ready for that kind of shift. I was ordained at twenty-eight and that was my first job. My first Sunday a parishioner asked the rector if my mom had to drive me to church. Her point was that I looked young. Too young. Young enough that it made her uncomfortable. Yet within four years we had a thriving program, and two members of the vestry were in their twenties, which was unthinkable to the organization even when I was hired.

After my work in young adult ministry, I was called to serve as the vicar of a church immediately following the founder's departure. I could write a whole book on following the founder of a church plant, but one thing that is safe to say is that even in the best of circumstances there is massive cultural change after a founder leaves. One of the things the church was known for was the clarity of its core values. The founder would literally read them out loud before every church service. They were integrated in the logo and all over every communication the church sent out. My second Sunday a longtime member asked, "What are our core values going to be now?" I was shocked, and uncomfortable. A strong sense of core values was one of the reasons I was attracted to the church in the first place. What I learned over time is that despite a herculean effort by the founder to instill a set of core values as he planted the organization, they had never really taken root. I couldn't find a single member who could correctly list the four values of the church. No matter how intentional, a church plant will always reflect the founder, which means when there is a transition, there is a vacuum and a whole new culture to change and grow.

Collaborative work is key to creating cultural change. **It is much easier to get people to remember what *they* say than it is to get them to remember what *you* say**. Corporate environments can get away with less collaboration and more specialization because people are motivated by their paychecks. Nonprofit management requires much more collaboration because participation is voluntary. Churches require even more collaborative leadership than other nonprofits because our goal is transformation.

I cannot tell you how many clergy have told me, "Oh, if I could only find a healthy parish." In my experience most church leaders feel victimized by the culture that they are in and have little idea how to change it. I would submit that is because we trap ourselves in denial. Clergy are often trained to see themselves as separate from the system and its dysfunction. We all know the myths that hold churches back.

"We want to grow but not change."

"We tried that and it didn't work."

"Young people today are just self-centered and lazy."

"We can't try anything too edgy or we might lose the few people we have."

The problem with myths is that contradicting them does little if any good. They become deeply ingrained in the organizational psyche, so much so that fighting them becomes nearly impossible and has led many clergy on the path to burnout. **Organizational myths cannot be contradicted, but they can be subverted.** What does that mean? Let me give oversimplified examples of both.

Contradicting an Organizational Myth

Congregant: Young people today are just self-centered and lazy.

Pastor: It isn't fair to say that. Look at Ian from the youth group. He gets up early every Saturday during the summer just to cut the church's lawn.

Congregant: I am not talking about Ian. I am talking about young people today.

Pastor: Ian is fourteen.

Congregant: I know that. I don't need a math lesson. I am saying kids don't care. There may be a few exceptions, but in general the youth of today care more about their Insta-whatever than they do about church or anything else.

Pastor: I think that is a dangerous attitude. I think that if kids like Ian heard that, they wouldn't want to come here. I don't think it would be safe here for them, so I would appreciate it if you didn't talk that way around here. You do want the church to grow, right?

Congregant: Yes, Reverend. I guess you are right.

(Fifteen minutes pass. The congregant is in the parking lot. The pastor has gone. The congregant sees Betty, the chair of the altar guild.)

Congregant: Betty! So good to see you.

Betty: Good to see you. It has been so long.

Congregant: It has.

Betty: How's it going?

Congregant: Good. *(laughs)* Though I just got a talking-to from the pastor.

Betty: Really? What about?

Congregant: I don't know. Some MSNBC craziness. I don't know if he will last. He is really out of touch with the congregation.

Betty: You think?

Congregant: Yeah. He was like, "Kids like Ian are important and old farts like you aren't."

Betty: He called you an old fart?

Congregant: Not in so many words, but yeah.

Subverting an Organizational Myth

Congregant: Young people today are just self-centered and lazy.

Pastor: Hmm, why do you say that?

Congregant: In general, the youth of today care more about their Insta-whatever than they do about church or anything else.

Pastor: So, you are saying, it used to be different.

Congregant: Sure did. I was in a youth group every Wednesday and church every Sunday.

Pastor: Church attendance sure has changed.

Congregant: World's going to hell in a handbasket.

Pastor: I think that a lot. . . . There are some good kids, though.

Congregant: Yeah?

Pastor: I was up here on Saturday morning at 8 a.m., and you know that kid Ian?

Congregant: Phil's boy? Yeah, he is what? About eleven?

Pastor: He is fourteen now.

Congregant: Shoot. They grow up quick.

Pastor: It is a good thing too. That kid has some muscles. Like I was saying I was up here at 8 a.m. and he had already mowed the whole church lawn.

Congregant: Really?

Pastor: Yep, he does it every week during the summer. He gets up early to do it. When I was fourteen you couldn't pay me to get up before 11 a.m.

Congregant: Not me. My daddy had us up at 6:00 a.m. every day.

Pastor: Really?

Congregant: Yep.

Pastor: Well, say what you will about the youth of today, but Ian ain't lazy.

Congregant: No he ain't. That is a good boy. He comes to church.

Pastor: He comes to church? Is that why you say kids are lazy, because they don't come to church?

Congregant: Absolutely, back in my day if I didn't have my butt in a pew, my pa would have tanned it.

Pastor: So, *(smiling)* you didn't want to be in church either? Not if your dad had to threaten you to go.

Congregant: Well . . . no I guess not.

Pastor: *(playfully)* Maybe kids haven't changed. Maybe you're just a little jealous.

Congregant: Ha! Maybe you're right. *(Sees Betty off in the distance)* Ooo. There is Betty. I haven't talked to her in a month. I should go.

Pastor: Ok, see you soon.

Congregant: Will do. Oh, and next time I see Ian I will give him a thank you. Those lines look great.

(Congregant catches up to Betty out of earshot of the pastor.)

Congregant: Betty!

Betty: Well hey stranger! Good to see you. You were talking to the pastor.

Congregant: Just a little. Hey, did you know that Ian kid gets up early to cut the church lawn? That is a good kid.

Yes, I know it's oversimplified, but the point is that when you fight over reality, you rarely get anywhere. Change is made when you get alongside someone. **More often than not in Christian leadership you will be asked to make a stand. That can be good, but making change is better.**

I had a mentor priest that did something that used to drive me crazy. Before every vestry meeting she would first put down her stuff at a chair. I would usually decide where I was going to sit relative to her. Then right before the meeting began she would pick up her stuff and move to a different spot. She did this every time.

One day she told me why. She said that if someone felt in conflict with her, they would subconsciously pick the seat opposite. She moved so that she would be next to that person instead of across from them. At first that seemed like overkill to me, but over the years I have been in some bad meetings, and I have noticed that when people argue across from each other, it escalates quickly. I am not sure if being across from the person is triggering, or if when you are fighting with someone next to you, you can't ignore how frustrated everyone else at the table is that there is a fight. In any case, "Yes, &" is the dialogue equivalent of sitting next to someone. Choosing to live inside the other person's reality, even if only for a short time, gets you past the standoff and to the conversation. Culture rarely changes as much as it did in the example with just one conversation but talking with someone will beat talking against them nine times out of ten.

I have come to believe that contrary to the lived consensus, changing a culture is not hard. There may be some genuine exceptions to that rule, but my guess is that there are far fewer than most church leaders think. Culture change is actually happening all the time. Harnessing it only requires two things: consistent trust building, and playful "Yes, &." You probably got the sense in the second example that the pastor wasn't just technically "Yes, &"-ing, he was doing it playfully: "So, you didn't want to go to church either." That is not just an "&," but a call back to the earlier statement.

"Maybe kids haven't changed. Maybe you are just a little jealous." That is a justification, but a playful one. Playfulness in dysfunctional systems takes immense discipline, but it is also incredibly fruitful. **Dysfunction is a perverse game. It cannot be dismissed or outfought. It can only be outplayed.** The improv process of "yes" allows the minister to enter into the worldview of the existing community. Then the creative instinct of "&" means that you don't get stuck there. This is how you subvert the myths on the ground. But I reiterate: if you are going to be playful and creative when people are saying things that attack your values, *you need to practice.* You need to train your brain to embrace the inherent awkwardness of those conversations.

Many will point to the pastor's integrity in the first example. He is right, after all. It is terrible and unwelcoming to say that about youth. You are correct. And there is a time to stand up against bad thinking, but how many times did Jesus turn over the tables in the temple? One. How many times did he bring his opponents in with a parable? Lots. God so loved the world that Jesus gave up the glories of heaven to meet us in our sin. Can we love our fellow Christians enough to give up the glory of being right all the time?

I firmly believe that if you master these skills and maintain a playful attitude, you can change the fundamental culture of any organization. Some will take longer than others, but we need not be victims of church culture anymore. With practice and time, we can shape the culture we have to be more loving and reflective of Christ.

Now, whenever I hear a priest say, "If I could only find a healthy church," I say, "Why? You want to retire? Healthy churches are already healthy. They don't need you. That would be a waste of your talents."

Exercise: Myth Busting

List three organizational myths that you have heard in churches and drive you bananas.

1. _____

2. _____

3. _____

Now write dialogues like the examples I gave. Start with the congregant delivering the actual quote. In my example it was, "Young people today are just self-centered and lazy." Write the dialogue contradicting the myth first. Then write one subverting it. If you have a friend to do this exercise with, it would be good to have them play the congregant. •

More Resources to Train as an Agent of Culture Change

One of the things I love about the church after Pentecost is that a person doesn't have to be important to lead important change. They don't have to be clergy or a vestry member or anything like that. The more that we exhibit a playful "Yes, &," the more the culture will change around us. As I have pointed out, these practices take practice, so the rest of this chapter is dedicated to mind games that are designed to help us step down from the judgment seat and toss away the whack-a-mole mallet in favor of cultivating curiosity and connection. These are a few things I do to stay rooted in the more organic staking-a-tomato-plant model of community. Put in another (very seminary) way: these exercises are designed to help you turn from institutional thinking to missional thinking.

First, let's start with a couple of exercises. I highly recommend that you move around and walk at this stage. We are going to jump into some parables after the exercises, so it's a good idea to engage your body, not just your mind.

Exercise: Wrong Name

Find a room you can be loud in. Set a timer for five minutes. Walk around the room. Every time you see an object, say a word (preferably a noun) that is NOT related to the thing you are looking at, and say it out loud. After the five minutes are up, answer the following questions:

- How did that feel?
- Did the feeling of the exercise change through the beginning, middle, and end?
- Did you ever start to feel like you could trust your instincts to come up with something random? •

Exercise: Failure Bow

Failure is way underrated. No one learns to walk without first learning how to fall one hundred different ways. Without the willingness to fail, improv doesn't work. Take a look at the cross. The same thing is true of Christianity. Improvisers teach themselves to celebrate failure in all kinds of ways, one of which is the failure bow. Like most improv exercises, failure bows are best perfected in a group setting, but you can do them on your own too.

Step 1: Make a failure bow. There needs to be a grandiose action and a loud vocalization. Remember this is a celebration. Usually for the vocalization I use the words, "I failed!"

Step 2: Set yourself up to fail. Do something that you won't be able to keep up forever. For example, name all of the fruits, or types of cars, or action heroes. Once you run out, do a failure bow.

Step 3: Create a shorthand failure bow. Take something about your unique failure bow and make a symbol that you could do without anyone else noticing. If your failure bow is that you strike a John Travolta disco pose, maybe the shorthand is just one finger pointing up. For the next week, every time you feel like you are failing, do your shorthand bow to remind you to embrace the awkward beauty of putting yourself out there. •

Exercise: Reflection Parable

Each parable goes through the improv process of "Yes, &." Parables begin by affirming the limited, broken, or even sinful perspective of the world. That is the "yes"—the radical acceptance of the reality the other presents. Then, the parable adds another element and creates tension with the original worldview. This is the "&." Ultimately the most useful parables end up using the tension to turn the original worldview upside down. I call this point the "turnaround."

Let me start by revisiting a parable I have already talked about: the good Samaritan. Here is an oversimplified example of one of Jesus's parables and how it uses the "Yes, &" model. In the parable of the good Samaritan, Jesus is responding to the question, "Who is my neighbor?" The worldview on the ground is that we have a duty to our neighbors, and holy people keep that duty but only to those to whom it is required. In the parable, Jesus accepts that worldview at first. He tells a story about one of "us" getting in trouble. *Ooh,* thinks the listener, *this is good. The one who helps the man or who is supposed to help the man will tell me the only people I am required to worry about.* Then Jesus goes to "&"—he picks holy and respectable people and has them walk right past the suffering man. This creates tension. *If a priest or a Levite isn't helpful, then is no one required to be?* becomes the troubling thought. Then a Samaritan, a reject and a religious half-breed to the audience, comes by and shows overwhelming generosity. Jesus asks his audience, "And who is a neighbor to this man?" The answer is painfully obvious. But the racial tension is so thick the audience can't even make themselves say, "The Samaritan," so they merely grumble out, "The one who showed mercy." Jesus responds, "Go and do likewise." This is the turnaround. It isn't about the mercy you owe; it is about the mercy you show. Don't worry about who counts as your neighbor: go and be a neighbor. To summarize the parable of the good Samaritan:

> Yes: We owe charity to certain people. Let's identify
> exactly who so that we can "count as righteous."
> &: Being "holy" by the rules doesn't necessarily mean
> you are charitable.
> Turnaround: Don't focus on the minimum of who you
> are required to serve. Serve and give abundantly.

Parables are complex and nuanced things. If my example seems overly simplistic, it is.

But hopefully this shows that parables are a tool to change not just someone's mind or actions, but how they see the world. (I mean, it worked for Jesus, right?)

Missional ministry serves the mission of God through engaging the needs of the wider community. Institutional ministry, which is much more common, is the unconscious process of serving the mission of the church establishment by leveraging the assets of the wider community. Missional ministry requires not only a different way of acting, but a different way of seeing ministry than many traditional models.

I wrote the following two parables to help readers understand the missional perspective. As you read them, attempt to identify the "yes," the "&," and the turnaround.

• • •

The Parable of the Dance

There was a certain man who lived in the 1960s. He owned and operated a ballroom dance hall. In the man's youth, the hall had been quite successful, which had pleased him greatly. You see, the man loved ballroom dance, and he loved to watch others discover its beauty and perfection.

But by the end of the sixties, things had changed. The man had long since become a father and a grandfather, and his beautiful hall was near empty. The youth of that day, for whatever reason, would no longer gather in ballrooms, and the man faced the difficult prospect of a failing business in his old age. To make matters worse, not even his own grandson would come to the dances anymore.

After he had felt sorry for himself long enough, the man discovered conviction. He would not and could not let the ballroom fail—not even because of the money, but because he knew deep down in his heart that the dance was too beautiful and too marvelous to be allowed to die with his generation.

He called his grandson and asked, "Why is it that young people like you don't come to the dances anymore?" The grandson replied, "Well, Grandpa, most of my friends don't even know the steps, and ..."

But the man cut him off midsentence—"That's it? That is easy. I can fix that."—and he hung up the phone to begin his work.

The man made a huge banner that read "Free Ballroom Lessons" and hung it across his building; then he waited expectantly. The man hired some more instructors because he expected such a volume of new students. And they waited ... and waited. But no one new showed up.

The next day, the man called his grandson a second time, and asked, "I offered classes. I don't get it. Why don't you young people come and dance anymore?"

The grandson replied, "Well, Grandpa, we do dance. We dance in soda shops and ice cream parlors. Sometimes we even dance in the streets to the rhythm of car radios, and ..."

The man cut him off in midsentence—"That's it? That's easy. I can fix that."—and he hung up the phone to begin his work.

The man made flyers, and he hung them up near soda shops and ice cream parlors, and he even taped some to sidewalks and in the streets. The fliers said, "Come dance in a ballroom hall. A beautiful place for *real* dancing." And the man went back to his hall. He waited ... and waited. But no one new showed up.

Frustrated, this time the man went to speak to his grandson in person. And he asked, "What am I doing wrong? I offered classes. I offered space. Why won't you young people come to dance at my hall?"

The grandson replied, "Well, Grandpa, we usually dance to completely different kinds of music. We dance to rock and roll, and besides ..."

The man cut him off midsentence. "That's it! This is too hard. How am I going to fix this? It doesn't make any sense. These dances are so beautiful, and so much fun. Why doesn't your generation care? Why don't you care? How could you let the dance die?"

The grandson looked up at the man's eyes. They were old and beautiful and red with tears. The grandson said, "Grandpa, please listen to me. I love you with all I have, and I hate to have to tell you this. I hate every word of it because I know how it breaks your heart, but I think you deserve the truth. And the truth is that no matter how much I want to, I don't trust your opinion on dancing. I can't. At least, not until you show me that you don't care about steps, and you don't care about the room, and you don't care about music as much as you care about the fact that I am already dancing."

The Parable of the Young Priest: An Apocryphal Prologue to Revelation

The young priest was getting some well-deserved rest after his ordination that day. He awoke to sounds of sobbing in his room. All the doors and windows were locked. In the dark he could barely make out a figure hunched over and crying in the southeast corner of the room.

"Can I help you, sir?" The young priest spoke sheepishly into the darkness.

"I am sure you cannot," rang out a snot-soaked voice from the corner. "Your bullshit kind never does. You will just cast me away without hearing me out."

"My kind?" said the young priest. "I don't know what you are talking about, but I promise to listen."

"Yes. Your kind: priests," said the figure as he began to stand. "I always visit you on your ordination night."

The figure stood tall and powerful. It was clear that it wasn't quite human.

Gripped with terror, the priest said, "You're . . . you're . . ."

"Yeah, yeah, I am Satan, the Prince of Darkness, the Devil, the Boogie Man, or whatever you want to call me."

The young priest gulped. Then he grabbed the cross around his neck, but before he could speak, Satan pointed his long red finger and scraggly fingernail at him and said, "You promised to hear me out."

The young priest stood in a defensive stance, thought for a quick beat, and said, "Okay, then."

"Really?" said Satan in disbelief. "That has never worked before. No one else has ever trusted me before."

"I didn't exactly say I trusted you," the young priest replied.

But Satan cut him off. "I can't believe I am finally going to get a chance to say this, but I want to repent."

"*You* want to repent?" said the young priest. "I feel like this is a trap."

"I am sure it is," said Satan, "but not for you. I have been trying to repent for two thousand years."

"Okay—umm—if so, then why didn't you say anything?"

Satan heaved a large breath and boomed, "Why didn't I say anything? What do you mean? I have been doing everything I can think of to try to get you stupid people's attention. I even visit every priest on their ordination night hoping to finally get one who will listen to me without trying to make a deal for themselves."

"Why would you, the King of Hell, want to repent?"

"The King of Hell? Ha! What good is a crown if it is so heavy it causes you to drown? You forget, boy, I was an angel. I used to hear God's song, hell, I used to sing the melody line, but now I can barely remember what that song felt like, much less the notes."

"I don't believe you," the young priest said. "You are a master of lies."

"I knew it! See, no guts, no commitment in your kind. Oh, and for the record I don't lie, I just don't stop you from lying to yourself."

But somewhere in the midst of the unholy anger, the priest caught a glimpse of the pain in the Devil's eyes, and found a surprising compassion for him. The young priest felt a cool wind on his face and could swear it whispered to him, "Evil cannot be destroyed, but it can be reconciled."

"Okay, I can't believe this, but I will do it," the priest said as he sat on the edge of the bed and grabbed his bag from underneath.

"You are going to take my confession?" Satan asked.

"Yep," said the young priest.

"Who do you think you are kidding?" the Devil said. "I am Satan. We both know that you aren't going to do this. We both know what I took from you."

A little startled, the young priest took a deep breath. Inhaled, exhaled, and replied, "Yes, we do, and yes, I will." Then the priest reached into his bag and grabbed a prayer book and a stole. He placed the purple vestment over the back of his neck, and thus it began.

That was the beginning of the end. •

Chapter 11

Group Mind and the Holy Spirit

The most mystical element in the improv community is a thing referred to as "group mind." For those who have not experienced this, it may seem artsy or made up, but every improviser I have ever learned from talked about its existence as a fact because once experienced, group mind is undeniable.

Sometimes when a group is on stage, especially a group that is well trained and plays together well, they start thinking as a unit. Someone will set up a joke and someone else will pick up the punchline immediately. It is not that individuality is lost. It is that each player keys into what the rest of the group is doing so deeply that there is an instinct that moves them all. Call anyone you know who has done high-level improv. It is real. It sounds crazy, but it is true.

There is a fantastic movie about a group of improvisers called *Don't Think Twice*.[1] I had an embarrassing moment when I watched it in the theater. I will confess that I am a huge fan of comedian Mike Birbiglia. When I watched his special *My Girlfriend's Boyfriend* I cried

---

1. Mike Birbiglia., dir, *Don't Think Twice* (Universal City, CA: Universal Pictures Home Entertainment, 2016).

because, while it was completely secular, it was the closest thing I had ever seen to what I have been trying to do with preaching my whole career. It was silly, insightful, vulnerable, and above all, loving. You can imagine that when I heard that he had written a movie about improvisers, I was all in. But it was a limited release, and I live in the most suburban suburb in the world.

I was set to drive over a hundred miles to see this movie when it came to an indie theater in Houston. For reference, that is a thirty-minute drive without traffic and a two-and-a-half-hour drive with it—not an exaggeration. I made my way to a weekday matinee.

The theater clearly was on its last leg. It looked like it had probably been quite lovely in its day. I'm sure it was the perfect place to watch the first run of *Casablanca*, but I don't think they had fixed a thing in it since. I saw three different chairs wrapped in caution tape and the room carried a slight smell, but I didn't care. I knew what I was about to see would be life-changing, but first, it was embarrassing. Luckily, my embarrassment was contained because there were only two other people in the theater and each of us was sitting alone.

At one point in the movie, one of the characters, Samantha, who loves improv more deeply than anything, was told by the guy running the theater that she needed to teach a level one class. The guy in charge had been teaching it, but decided that he wanted to spend more time focusing on forwarding his career. Samantha was in her head about teaching, but in true improv form she decided to go for it. In her first class she stood up in front of the students. This was an awesome moment to watch as an improviser because Samantha was dripping with awkwardness, as if she had channeled all the natural level one awkwardness into herself.

After a few awkward lines Samantha said, "What did I want to talk to you about? . . . *(She bends up and down thinking.)* I wanted to talk to you about . . . group mind." She kept talking at that point, but I missed it all because I was laughing so hard and for so long that no one heard anything for the rest of the scene. It was bad, folks. I was pretty sure I was going to break my chair and make them wrap another seat in caution tape. And I was the only one laughing. I was mortified, but I couldn't stop. If I had any decency at all, I would have paid the other two patrons back for their tickets.

I knew why I was laughing so hard, and I knew why no one else was getting the joke. It was because I am an improviser. Group mind is an advanced concept. To walk in to a level one class and open with it is truly hilarious. It would make the teacher look crazy, which Samantha did, and I probably do now. But it is a real thing. Over time, as you play with an improv group you get to the point where you feel something like a person-to-person energy telling you whom to let take the focus and when to give it away.

Part of the reason I found the scene so funny has to do with the character. Samantha is the most idealistic improviser of the film. She just loves the art of it, and the free-flowing support of one another is her favorite thing about improv. Of course, she tried to teach that in her first level one class, and of course it went terribly.

Basic Group Mind Exercise

While group mind is an elusive and high-level skill for an improv community to develop, there are some basic things that groups will do to work on it. One of them is a counting game. This is something that I strongly recommend doing with church leadership groups like vestries, though it is very important that the group has already reached the point where there is enough trust that they are not afraid to look stupid in front of each other. It is a great thing to do, for example, if you have already mastered failure bows[2] or something similar.

The game is simple. Bring everyone in shoulder to shoulder and tell them to look down or close their eyes. Ask the group to count to

---

2. See exercise in the previous chapter.

ten. Each number can come from anyone in the circle, but if two people say the same number at the same time, they have to start again back at one. Instruct the group to avoid creating patterns (like going around the circle) and to instead sense the time for each person to speak.

I did this exercise many times with many different groups and it made no sense to me—until finally something changed in me. It is so interesting how the game changes with experience. I have seen groups try for fifteen minutes and not get past four. I have seen groups blow past ten and make it to thirty on the first shot.

It reveals a great deal about a group. Who hangs back for fear of messing it up? When does the group go slow? Who tries to say their number superfast to make sure they have a chance to get one in?

Over time in this exercise, you stop listening to the voices and start feeling the energy in the room. I began to know where in the circle the next number was going to come from before anyone spoke. You get to the point that when two people say a number at the same time, you know who was speaking from anxiety and whose turn it really was. Or sometimes you can even tell who was supposed to speak but didn't so two other people ran into the void. It is strange, but it can become a truly mystical practice, and the experience helps create a kind of community that is both light and ineffable. •

Group Mind by Another Name

As a priest I have a different name for group mind: it has become clear to me that this group mind is what Christians call an experience of the Holy Spirit. We believe that in the sanctified community the Holy Spirit, the very presence of God, has been set loose. The Spirit can and does speak through anyone drawn to our circle. This belief is central to true Christianity. It is what makes the difference between a living Christian faith and the morally judgmental Deism that so often masquerades as the official American religion. God is here and God is working in us, or perhaps it is better to say, **the Holy Spirit isn't**

just at work; she is at play. I said in chapter 7, play is the best teacher I know. It is a necessary instinct for survival. It is the most efficient way to learn anything, and learning through play makes us want to learn more.

I have heard countless sermons and pretended to read countless books about how God is at work in the world, but I have seen almost nothing about how God is playing with us. But how else can we make sense of this gospel in our hands? How else can we make sense of a God so feared that even Moses wouldn't look him in the face deciding, "You know what? I am going to become human by being born of a peasant girl." How else do we make sense of a teacher like Jesus who is constantly poking not just at the establishment but at his own disciples with parable after parable that reveal the ridiculousness of human prejudice and powerbroking?

As an Episcopalian, I have to laugh because how else can we make sense of a God who would continue to play along, join, and inspire us as we prance around in robes, bow, kneel, and share a snack? The dress-up games we play with our clergy are humorous. I can't believe a maniple exists, much less that I know the name for it. And yet, despite or perhaps because of its ridiculous peculiarity, God shows up. The Holy Spirit gives nurture, insight, and direction, and teaches us what it means to be a Christian in these, our bizarre communities. **In a world where only power and work are taken seriously, maybe the only true way for love and blessing to emerge is through something as utterly ridiculous as the divine liturgy.**

Don't Give Up on My Irreverence

I hope you know by now that I joke because I love. In fact, I poke fun at my tradition like it is my little brother because we are family. I say that, and yet one of the crucial points I am trying to make about faith is that **when you remove the silly, the sarcastic, and the playful, the gospel itself slips through your fingers.**

Crumbs on the Floor

Let me give you a real-life example that is painfully ironic to me. And I do mean painfully. This story hurts to tell and I think it is funny at the same time. I don't know if you know, but a seminary graduation is a big to-do. It is all the seriousness and formality of a grad school graduation wrapped in a special church service with a guest speaker. The students who aren't graduating that year are often given the responsibility for planning and executing much of the event, which is high stakes because they are also saying goodbye to their friends whom they want to honor.

My second year (of three) at seminary, the pressure on graduation rose exponentially. The Most Rev. Katharine Jefferts Schori was the guest preacher for the affair. She had recently become the first woman to serve as the presiding bishop, which is the highest-ranking cleric in the Episcopal Church. People were abuzz with excitement and anxiety. We had no idea how to estimate how many people would be coming, and none of us wanted to turn anyone away from worshiping God or hearing such an historic figure in our church.

It was an all-hands-on-deck situation for our student body. Everyone had a job. Most of us were labeled "sacristan" and dressed in black cassocks (robes) so we could usher and assist in all kinds of ways. This was especially important because it was a communion service. Given that we didn't know how many people were coming, we had to create a circuitous plan for making sure that everyone would be near enough a station to receive the bread and wine quickly and efficiently.

One other thing happened that year that is important to the story. The faculty and students went through an exhaustive process regarding the bread we used for communion. One of the first-year students had celiac disease, so we had decided as a community that we would use only gluten-free bread for communion. That way no one was at risk and we were all sharing the same bread. (Apparently that decision is controversial in some circles, which I still don't understand.) It also was the tradition for our graduation to use baked loaves rather than wafers for communion. Put those two things together and we needed a new recipe for bigger gluten-free loaves. Gluten is sticky. It's what keeps most bread from crumbling too much and falling apart. As you might have guessed, our meal with Jesus that day got a little messy. By "a little messy," I mean that the area around the communion stations looked like the circle of destruction around a high chair at Cracker Barrel, which was fine at every single station—but one.

In line at one of the stations was a priest that none of us knew. He was obviously upset about the crumb situation. For those of you who don't know, in the Episcopal tradition we treat the bread and wine of communion with great respect after it has been blessed. We do our best to honor every crumb and every drop. The bread and wine are to be either consumed or buried, which is why every Episcopal church comes with a special sink that goes straight into the ground rather than into the sewer so that we can properly dispose of any extra wine. I think this is a good practice. It is a discipline that both fills us with a sense of mystery about the profound communion with God we get through Holy Communion (redundancy intentional), and also trains us with a focus for the holy that hopefully will affect the way we see everything in life.

That, however, doesn't excuse what happened. After receiving communion himself, the incensed priest began trying to scoop up the crumbs. A student from my seminary serving as a sacristan strained to aid him. She joined him on the floor trying in vain to save every crumb. Never mind that the perseverating priest was literally blocking the line of people waiting to receive communion, but he also exploded in anger at the student who came to help him. He was so vehement it brought her to tears—and that took some doing. She was a tough woman who had been through a lot and was just trying to help.

Let's recap the pastoral leadership of this anonymous priest. For him, the dignity of the Eucharist became so important that he blocked people's access to the very thing he valued. Then he verbally attacked an innocent person who was trying to help him without being asked. I honestly hope and pray that was that man's worst day, that his behavior came out of some unbelievable stressor and he ran to God for forgiveness and grace. In any event, that day he put his attachment to the sacrament above the purpose of the sacrament: to make us more Christlike.

I don't mean to make this person I don't know into a two-dimensional villain. People make mistakes for lots of reasons, which is why it is important to find the distance and insight that levity can bring. When we can, we start to "get" the Bible differently. The Sadducees were the religious leaders who ran the temple that was the center of Jewish worship. They were so wrapped up in what they thought God wanted that they saw Jesus as a threat. Just as I don't think I should make the priest in this story two-dimensional, I don't think we should pigeonhole the Sadducees. The frustrating thing is that they share what looks like religion, but it is really religiosity— something none of us is immune from falling into. **Religiosity is about control. Religion is about partnership with God.** If we take our faith seriously, we need to come to terms with the fact that we have an inner crumb-gathering priest. Play is our soul's natural defense against all the things that might rob us of the joy and wonder of the Holy Spirit alive and present in each unique moment.

Religiosity is the constant temptation of the religious, so, sadly, the religious can easily become the most alienated and even violently opposed to what our mysterious and living God is doing. A ridiculous percentage of text in the Gospels is dedicated to poking fun at this irony. Until we see the humor of it, we never really understand who Jesus of Nazareth is, or the incredible gift it is to be his disciple.

And if we are to form communities that make true disciples, our leadership also needs to exhibit that kind of lightheartedness.

The character of a community changes the character of its members. Playful and skillful "Yes, &" leadership is the best tool I know for creating community culture change for sure, but it simultaneously fosters change on the individual level as well. A grace-filled environment is the key to personal transformation that defines true discipleship.

SECTION

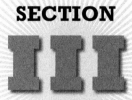

Character Work

Introduction

Now you have a sense of the kind of spontaneous, collaborative, loving, and spirit-centered leadership a community of disciples requires. It is as if you have learned all about the tree and its roots, so now you are hungry for its fruit. What does an experience like this do? What does it have to do with Jesus and making true disciples? Everything. Come see.

In this section, I will lay out some basic practices of discipleship from the individual's perspective. Section II was about creating a disciple-making community; this section first addresses the basics and then invites the reader to define discipleship themselves. I want this section to begin conversations in churches, coffeehouses, and Waffle Houses. I am not looking to supply a definition; I am encouraging you to think about discipleship anew given what we have experienced together so far.

Chapter 12

Commitment, Faith, and True Discipleship

[Jesus asked,] "What do you think? A man had two sons; he went to the first and said, 'Son, go and work in the vineyard today.' He answered, 'I will not'; but later he changed his mind and went. The father went to the second and said the same; and he answered, 'I go, sir'; but he did not go. Which of the two did the will of his father?" They said, "The first." Jesus said to them, "Truly I tell you, the tax collectors and the prostitutes are going into the kingdom of God ahead of you." (Matt. 21:28–31)

Faith and Certainty

I hate it when people talk about "blind faith." Faith opens our eyes. It is about what we can see, not about what we pretend. Somewhere in the American religious tradition, faith came to mean intellectual certainty. When that happened, doubt was seen as the opposite of faith, but biblically that is not true at all. When God told Moses, "Go to Pharaoh," do you think God cared if along the way Moses wondered whether the burning bush was God talking or the result of eating

153

some day-old hummus? No. Faith was not in the thinking. Faith was in the walking. The need for certainty is an invention of modernity. Early Christian scholars noted contradictions in the Bible. No one found them disturbing until the rise of fundamentalism. That is why the ancient creeds of the Church say nothing about believing that the Bible is inerrant. The question was irrelevant because early Christians understood one simple thing: faith isn't about certainty. It is about commitment. Put another way, **the opposite of faith isn't doubt. The opposite of faith is bailing**.

Attack the Stage

When I was in high school, I had a friend on the football team. I told him I didn't know how I could ever be on the line because I would know I was going to get hit each time.

"I think I would be tempted to pull back," I said.

"That would be a bad idea," he said. "When you hit them with everything you've got, you are fine; it is when you hold back that you get hurt."

I don't know much about football, but there is a lot in life where the instinct to protect ourselves can do way more harm than good. I remember teaching each of my sons how to catch a baseball. His first instinct was to close his eyes and turn his head away. The problem was, that was more dangerous. It is way harder to catch or even evade a ball if your eyes are closed.

Improv is much the same way. There is a tremendous temptation to hold back and try to look cool, but there are some problems with that strategy. The audience can see or feel the energy on the stage. If the energy dies every time it comes to you, it doesn't matter how cool you look, they will resent you and they won't even know why. The reason the scene stalls when it comes to you is because your ego is standing in the way of the scene. One of the pieces of advice often given to improvisers is "Attack the stage." That means to come with full energy to the performance and act as if you have no fear of being seen.

Don't Think Twice

Earlier I mentioned the movie *Don't Think Twice* by Mike Birbiglia. One of the golden nuggets in that movie is an illustration of how trust is broken in a group because of ego. Improv is a beautifully collaborative art form, but showbiz isn't. This movie plays with the dynamics of an incredible improv troupe in which each member of the group is equally talented, yet one player "makes it" and the others don't.

At one point in the movie, the troupe, called "The Commune," is playing a set when a group from a *Saturday Night Live*–like TV show sends a talent scout to watch for people to invite to audition. One of the players bends a scene in a way that allows him to do his best impression of President Obama. It is funny and subtle to the outsider, but everyone on the team knows he is showboating. The player tries to make himself look good rather than focusing on the thing that they are making together. There is even a great scene after the show where the troupe gives the show-off a hard time and he admits that he went too far. It was a fun and playful exchange about friends making up. But then the showboater gets an audition. So does a woman who is just in love with improv and would be happy to be playing with these people forever. The rest of the group, not so much.

Like Adam tasting the apple, this poisons the group's innocence and leads to mistrust. The woman self-sabotages by skipping the audition altogether; maybe deep down she knows what she wants, and it is the improv community rather than fame. The showboater gets the part on the TV program. He is gradually disappearing from the group, but there are several shows after that. Over a short period of time, all the players start subtly slipping as performers. They start ignoring suggestions that have to do with the showboater's success; eventually they start all out denying them (failing to say "yes" to the reality they are given). The quest for success continues to lead to tension between group members until there is only one left to perform for their last show. Eventually the characters find ways to move past the need for success and they reconcile, but the showboater has to walk away with a twinge of regret because he misses the fun and high-quality comedy that was being made in the environment of collaboration.[1]

I tell this story because it is a beautiful example of what happens when people start playing for themselves, or protecting themselves. By showboating, the one improviser was protecting himself at the expense of the group. He was making himself look good. On the flip side, after the trust was broken, the other improvisers held back, which is also a way of protecting the ego. This fractured the trust and all of the performers lost the fundamentals. When one person breaks the faith, it shakes the whole community.

Attack the Stage Reprised

Attacking the stage doesn't mean bowling people over. It is about bringing your full energy to your scene partners because when you do, it amps them up, which in turn amps you up more. Once I heard a person ask, "Why can't white preachers preach like Black preachers?"

A wise Person of Color retorted, "Because they don't have a Black congregation."

Experiencing preaching from the African American tradition is mesmerizingly wonderful to me, and it is a great example of the power that comes from attacking the stage. Seeing a great preacher from the Black church tradition is something else. Not only is the message inspiring, meaningful, and honest, the delivery is unique. The use of breath, pause, crescendo, and staccato is musical. The

---

1. Birbiglia, *Don't Think Twice.*

movements of the sermons become a dance between the preacher and the response of the congregation.

I once heard a story about a bookish seminary professor who went to preach in one of those churches. It was not going well. Everyone knew it. While the congregation was used to shouting acclamations of "Amen!" and "Preach!" there was barely a mumble. Then a woman's voice rang out from the congregation loud enough that the whole auditorium could hear: "Dear Lord, help him, Jesus!"

I have no idea what happened at that moment, but I hope the preacher cracked up. I hope the whole place laughed the tension away so they could move forward finding genuine meaning in the sermon. But the reason why I tell this story is not because of the outcome, it is because of what was going on in that woman. On the one hand, this story is hilarious to me because I can only imagine how horrifying it would be to have my sermon be called out in real time, but then think about that woman herself. If it is true that she said these things, what else must be true of her?

She seemed to believe that she was in part responsible for his "performance." She saw it as her role to let the preacher know when they were (or were not) on a roll. Moreover, her connection wasn't just to the preacher. This was an actual prayer. She expected that Jesus was listening and would help the preacher deliver the Word. While this is a funny anecdote, it is also an incredible example of how some communities see the act of preaching as an interactive process between the preacher, the congregation, and the divine.

The intense behavioral norms of many congregations stifle that. Most preachers are not taught to attack the stage, at least not in the Episcopal Church. Many of us were taught to preach in basically the same way we were taught to write a paper on a biblical topic—and it shows. But if we don't attack the pulpit, how can we expect our congregrants' thoughts on God to make it out of the parking lot?

I was blessed early in my career as a priest because I learned something terrifying: people are actually listening. It is hard to tell that from most congregations, but after my third sermon (several months into my first job) I was talking to a parishioner and the topic of my preaching came up. She went point for point through all three sermons as if she was working from my outline. I don't think I could have done that for my most recent sermon, and I had finished preaching only an hour before.

People are listening. The best thing you can do to make your preacher better is to make sure they know that. Not just, "Hey, nice sermon," but something specific. There is nothing more motivating to a preacher than realizing that they are not just preaching to themselves.

Another experience nearly brought me to tears. I was preaching on a Sunday when we also had an induction ceremony to the Order of the Daughters of the King, which is a group of women who commit themselves to prayer, service, and evangelism. It isn't a monastic order, but it is a scaled-back version of that. The Daughters at my church are great, and they love to do it up when they are inducting new members. Their order has a theme color, which is blue, so that Sunday the first four pews on the left were awash with smiling ladies in matching "Daughters' blue."

In the sermon that day I had an odd tangent about "orans position." If you have ever seen a priest celebrate communion, then you have seen orans position. It is an ancient posture of prayer where a person stands and stretches their arms out and up. It looks kind of like a football ref calling a field goal. In the sermon I was talking about all of the different positions to pray in, and how most of the time people only think of kneeling, which feels closed off; then I talked about how wide and open orans feels. I also mentioned offhand that in the early church it wasn't just the clergyperson who would stand in orans. The whole congregation would lift their hands as part of the tremendous celebration we call Holy Communion. Then I went about my priestly Sunday stuff.

When it came time for the communion prayer, I raised my hands as always into orans. However, this time I was not alone. About 40 percent of the congregation joined in, including all of the Daughters in those beautiful blue front rows. I was in disbelief. The orans thing wasn't even my main point, it was just an aside. And these were Episcopalians. We do not like change, yet this group led by church ladies turned on a dime because they heard one thing that touched them.

I wish all preachers were more confident that our preaching really matters, because it does. When you know that, you commit so much more to showing up in prayerful power. I also wish all congregants were more confident in their job of letting the preachers know that their sermons matter and *how* they matter. I wish that clergy and congregations all knew that they are supposed to feed off each other's energy—that worship, prayer, service, evangelism, fellowship, and all the work of the church should be fun and engaging and demand our best playful selves.

Commitment, the spiritual equivalent of attacking the stage, is what God demands consistently in the Bible. How many of Jesus's stories or parables insist that when it comes to the kingdom of heaven we should be all-in? We would pay anything for that pearl. Our wholehearted devotion and zeal is the seal on our power, fulfillment, and our experience of grace—so give it all you got on the mission field. "For those who want to save their life will lose it, and those who lose their life for my sake will find it" (Matt. 16:25). Faith isn't about rejecting stray thoughts; it's about turning your whole life over to the source of life itself. That is counterintuitive. We think it is smart to play it safe, but when you hold back that is when you get hurt.

Chapter 13

Being Yourself on Stage

Finding Elusive Authenticity

One day in my improv class we did an exercise that I still wonder about. That week we were working on mime. Improvisers practice a great deal. It is invaluable. You never know what props or costumes you will need for the play being written and performed simultaneously. We have also discovered other interesting things about mime and how it grounds the imagination; it can be extraordinarily useful for inspiration and getting a performer out of their head. But teaching mime and teaching people to improvise can become a little too predictable. Before I talk about the exercise that changed my life, I first want to show you how much of a struggle it is to teach this basic skill.

Here is a scene from a hypothetical improv class. I don't *know* if this has ever happened exactly like I describe and yet I am sure that it has happened somewhere *exactly* like this.

Player 1 takes the stage. Begins to mime as if she is sweeping with a large industrial broom.

Player 2 enters.

Player 2: Hey, what are you sweeping there?

Improv teacher: Cut, cut. Ok. So, this time I want you to try to mime but not talk about the thing you are doing. People sweep all the time, but in real life when we see someone sweeping we don't generally talk about the sweeping. We talk about other things while we are doing the action. Everyone can see that she is sweeping.

Players 1 and 2: Oh! Ok.

Player 2: Good note, Coach.

Improv teacher: Ok, let's try it again.

Player 1 enters and begins sweeping as before.

Player 2: Hey, good morning. The sky is beautiful out today!

Player 1: Who can tell? I have just been sweeping all day. I haven't had a chance to even look up.

Improv teacher: Cut. Ok, that was actually a lot better. We still talked about sweeping [*nervous laughter*], but we know things now. It is a beautiful day. Player 1 is working tirelessly. We can be curious about why she is working so hard and Player 2 just seems oblivious. Now let's try it again with the same intro, but I want you to focus on the relationship of the characters you are playing. Remember there is no need to talk about the sweeping.

Player 1 enters for a third time sweeping in the same way.

Player 2: Gaby! My beloved wife. I am so glad to see you.

Player 1: Of course you are. All you ever do is be glad because I am always sweeping for you because you never lift a finger.

Improv teacher: Ok, that is scene.

What is interesting about that hypothetical class is that the improvisers were learning and growing as improvisers. It isn't bad to talk about what you are doing in improv and the second two scenes could easily have become something interesting to watch. It takes practice to separate the doing of an imaginary thing with the creation of imaginary dialogue.

I once had an improv class where the teacher tried a novel approach to teaching this skill, but it ended up revealing a lot to me about character and vulnerability.

The class went on stage two by two. Each group was given a suggestion of an environment for their scene: Kitchen. Airport. Frozen yogurt shop. High school gym. Then we were asked NOT to play a character. We were asked to mime an activity while we spoke as ourselves about what had happened over the weekend. I assumed that the teacher was trying to show that we could have a whole conversation without referencing the activity we were doing.

It was beautiful how terribly awkward these scenes were. Sometimes one of the players didn't realize they had slipped into playing a character, but you never really know. The teacher had to interject several times with questions like "Did you really have your high school reunion this weekend?" "Wait, you went to Africa and back two days ago?" "Somehow I doubt that you, Steve, graduated from clown college yesterday." It was as if several of my classmates had mental blocks and just couldn't hear the direction to be themselves.

We got through everyone's scenes. I really enjoyed mine. I liked taking the pressure off. As a pastor the question, "What did you do this weekend?" is kind of a nonstarter. The answer is always going to be, "I worked." But I enjoyed getting to be myself and not having to worry about the normal pressure of performing. We even got a few laughs, which I considered a bonus.

But after the exercise the teacher polled the class. "Who found it easier to mime when you weren't talking about it?" "Who found it harder?" She asked several questions but then got to one that was truly revealing. "Who found it easier to play as yourself than as a character on stage?" My hand shot up. I looked around and noticed that it was the only one. Becoming self-conscious I took it down. Then curiosity overtook anxiety for a second[1] and I said, "Wait, you find it easier to be a character?"

One of my friends said, "On stage? Yes." The rest of the class nodded. I was visibly befuddled.

Then my teacher said something deeply insightful. "You are a priest though, right?"

I said, "Yes."

"So, you are probably used to being yourself on stage." And she went on with class.

That stuck with me. "Am I used to being me? Or is there just a *me* character?" I have awful stage fright, especially when preaching. Every Sunday, I wonder to myself if this is the week I am not going to show up because I am so freaked out about preaching. It has been like that for twelve years. How could I be good at being myself? Until that moment I had never thought of church as a stage. Worship was categorically different in my mind. The fear was the same, but I never realized that it was the same fear and that it came from the same place.

Being Yourself Is Difficult

Eighth Grade[2] is a movie that follows the life of a girl named Kayla at the end of her eighth-grade year. One of my favorite monologues of all time comes from this movie. Kayla is making a video blog because social media is the primary way she meets the world. She is trying, like all eighth graders, to decide who she wants to be and emulate what she likes. Her video blog is about being pretty and popular and

---

1. Curiosity and anxiety perform such an elegant tango.
2. Bo Burnham, dir., *Eighth Grade*. (Santa Monica, CA: Artisan/Lionsgate, 2018).

living your fullest life.[3] The monologue is her trying to teach her audience how to be authentic. It is masterfully crafted because, without poking fun at her or her generation, the monologue has her talk about authenticity in a way that is so forced it is hysterical. I wonder what it would be like to watch that scene with the eighth graders in my youth group, especially the girls.

I am no expert on social media, and I am not interested in blasting it. To me it is a tool and like a hammer it can be used to build or injure. The omnipresence of social media breeds a level of self-consciousness that startles me. Once I was with friends I hadn't seen in a long time. I tried to grab a selfie because they were friends from different phases of my life and I wanted a memory of those times coming together. We were in a crowded auditorium. I pulled out my phone and held it straight in front of me to take the selfie. Immediately, I heard four people audibly gasp and two shout, "No!" They explained that I needed to hold the phone at a forty-five-degree angle or the photo would be unflattering. I was genuinely grateful for the kindness of those strangers, but it is telling that something as small as the potential of an unflattering photograph required an emergency response from those around. We try so hard to look authentic that sometimes we overtake it. We live in a world where it is difficult to know who you are, much less have the courage to be seen.

Knowing Your Character

When you play a character, it doesn't come with as much self-doubt, worry, or confusion as being yourself. You can hide behind the thing you are portraying and be both seen and hidden at the same time.

---

3. Videos about how to live your best life. You know, like everything on the internet that isn't how-to videos or cats, or well . . . things a pastor won't mention in print.

This is why my classmates found it easier to talk in character than it was to talk as themselves.

One of the things that the practices of improv reveal is that knowing your character speeds up everything. When you embody a character and let yourself go where it takes you, the journey becomes much less difficult. You don't have to weigh all the different options about what you can or can't say and do in a scene. Just put yourself through the filter of the character you are playing and make choices.

As an improviser, that advice was transformative for me. I don't have to be the author or the best scene partner. I need to have faith that if I play my character well, then the scene will come through better than I could have planned it. While that was great advice for me as an improviser, it has proven much more valuable for me as a Christian.

Respond versus React

When I talk about using the principles of improv to develop a Christian character, there is a significant tension that I would like to name. In improv we are often taught not to think. "Acting is react-ing" is a cliché in the theater world and even more in improv. We want you, we need you, to make a choice. That is what being a good partner means. Training yourself to be able to let the mind flow is one of the first things you cover in improv. Trusting your intuition is part of trusting yourself, and having a place where you can play uncensored is an essential part of finding authenticity either with the character you choose to play or with the Christian you choose to be.

This is counterintuitive for most contemporary spiritual leaders. For us the cliché is "Don't react, respond." We have been informed by therapy (which I deeply value) and family systems. Christians, and clergy especially, are trained to try to appear more virtuous than we are. We try to slow ourselves down, move out of our old (or emotional) brain and into our new (logical) brain. There can be a lot of value in that process but it sets us up to be fake. It sets us up to obscure doubt. It leads us to try to see without being seen, to love without ever trusting that we could be loved. It teaches us that we need to be something other than who we are in order to be effective and good. But remember the lesson of the tomato plant from chapter 5. Our calling should make us more of ourselves, not melt us down into something different. My pastoral education says respond out of the new brain, don't react out of the old one. The improviser in me quips back, "Old brain? New brain? That is all in your head. Get out of that." **Know your character. That will make your choices for you before you have a chance to mess them up.**

Exercise in Not Thinking

One of my favorite exercises in not thinking is called "Five Things." Get the group in a circle and someone poses a challenge to one player: "Give me five reasons why _____". The challenger can fill in the blank however they want. Five reasons why Houston summers are awesome. Five reasons why salamanders are the best pets. Five reasons you should never trust a man wearing suspenders. After the challenge is offered, the whole group says, "Ooh" to recognize the challenge. Then the one being challenged has to rapid-fire give five reasons for whatever. The answers don't have to be good or right or make sense. They just have to say something, and after each thing the ensemble yells enthusiastically, "Yes!" Once they get to five, everyone cheers. This teaches people to talk without thinking in an environment of unconditional support.

You can do this yourself to help you come up with new things but having a group of people to say Yes! is really an invaluable thing. Knowing the support is there will let you free yourself and will help you learn to trust yourself without thinking. This is an essential part of making creativity and character an authentic instinct rather than a stratagem. It seems nuts, but the less you think, the smarter, funnier, and more powerful you are. We are often afraid of what we will say when we let it all go. That is what knowing your character is for. •

The Stencil Lesson

I realize that this character stuff can seem counterintuitive so let me give you a metaphor that hopefully will help the message go down easier.

Recently I decided that I wanted to spruce up some things around our house. I knew that I would make my wife happy and, since this was written during the pandemic, I also realized that I needed something physical to get me out of my head and turn my excess energy into something useful. Our back porch is small and the paint on the concrete had worn out in some spots. We also have an artistically inclined six-year-old who is a joy to our hearts and a nightmare to nice things. My wife mentioned that she wanted the concrete repainted, which should have been easy enough, but it was way outside of my wheelhouse. This man is not handy. Carpenter is just a name. I have no practical skills at all, but for some reason I wanted to elevate the experience a little. I got it in my head to stencil the area where we keep our patio furniture. I saw something online where stenciled paint ended up looking like an outdoor rug.

It was much harder than I expected, but it turned out well. That gave me the courage to try some even more ambitious things inside the house. Once again, it was more difficult than I expected, but it turned out well. It is not uncommon for me to find a new obsession and stencils were mine for about two weeks.

The project outside spoke so easily to the improviser in me. Stenciling is imperfect. That is part of its beauty. I also figured that if the project outside failed, it would take me all of ten minutes to paint over it. **The freedom to fail blesses you with courage.** I went back with the original color after to clean it up and make it more to my design. To my surprise and delight I kept finding "accidents" that I liked more than the clean design, so I left them.

It was the project inside that tested me. I painted a dark blue stripe on an off-white wall and then planned to use the same off-white to stencil over the dark blue. For all my artist soul, actual drawing or painting is a nightmare for me. I literally can't draw a straight line with a ruler. Once I put dark paint on light paint, it wasn't an easy fix. It involved primer and more days of the kids staying away from wet paint.

There I was on my knees, painting and praying. The strip turned out well and I started stenciling. I got through the first two, but I didn't like how they looked, so I thought I was in trouble. The pattern was getting lost or obscured. On the stencil there were these clean lines and small dots, which really sold the mandala vibe, but after the first two, the lines and dots were too thick. If the whole thing was going to be like that, it wasn't going to work.

I wasn't ready to give up, so I painted another stencil in the line. This time I used much less paint. The lines seemed more faded, or even aged—in a good way. It looked the way I wanted it to look. I also realized that when I was finished I would have a problem. The first two wouldn't match and I would probably have to paint over them and do it again. Lining them up the second time would be a huge headache, but I knew I couldn't do anything until they dried, so I kept going.

As I continued, I got better at this less-paint affect. I found ways of making it look at least as nice and it started going much faster once I realized something else. In the beginning I tried to cover the holes of the stencil with paint. When I used less paint, I was still trying to paint the wall. Things got faster, more fun, and more beautiful when I realized that rather than trying to paint the wall through the stencil, I could just paint the stencil itself. When I did that, when I painted the stencil in broader strokes and started trusting it to filter what needed to be there, all of a sudden the excess paint was left on the outside of the stencil and what made it to the wall was just the right amount of paint.

Christian character is the stencil of life. It is the virtues and qualities of the person that God designed that will reveal the art underneath. It is when we decide to try to paint through or around the stencil that things get wonky. When we trust the stencil (God, your community, all of the things that support your faith life), then we can slather all of our passion and love onto our lives and know that the things that need to get through will and the excess can be left where it belongs. Painting the wall looks pretty, but it is still holding back. Playing our authentic character, however, makes us free to give all we have to God and discover the beauty we can make together.

Playing with characters in improv helps you discover that you can be more than one thing and that you can be more than one way. One minute you are a hateful conniving CEO, the next a damsel in distress, and the next a boy learning about life while fishing with his pa.

Personality is difficult if not impossible to change, but character is a different story. We have the character we have because of the choices we make and because of the communities that form us. The practice of making a character authentic to yourself and your call is usually more difficult than we expect, but it can turn out beautifully.

Epilogue to the Stencil Story

On the chance that any of you were concerned, let me tell you what happened with the first two unmatching stencils. As the vision of what I was looking for and the process clarified, I wondered more and more about those first two and what to do about them. Should I leave them there as an entry point to tell my story of transformation? That sounded good to me, but I wasn't sure my wife would want to look at that every day. Should I paint over them and risk the replacements being out of line?

I continued stenciling until I got to the end of the line. There was a place that wrapped around a corner and I couldn't decide if I wanted to wrap around with it. I decided to try, knowing it would be easy to paint over the light-colored stencil with the dark color of the stripe. I didn't like the way that one looked. On a whim, I swept the stencil brush that had very little of the dark paint on it over the excess stencil. I noticed that the light brushing gave the stencil more of the faded look that I had found when I used my more advanced method.

I went to the first two stencils, which were overly thick with the light paint, and I swept them with the dark paint, and they matched the rest. They even looked a little better than the others. Proof once again that **allowing yourself freedom to make mistakes, then giving yourself space to learn from them, can allow you to make something more beautiful than the original design.** How gospel is that?

Chapter 14

Finding Your Character

There are lots of ways of finding a character in improv. Most of them involve walking. I strongly recommend trying them for yourself (see this chapter's exercise). There is no better way to get critical distance on your worldview than by experimenting with another.

One of the clearest ways to make characters was described by an amazing improviser named Jill Bernard.[1] I saw Jill perform years ago and I am still laughing. She comes up with characters lightning fast. I saw her in the international ComedySportz competition when it was hosted in Indianapolis. I have a salient memory of one of the moments. They asked for a volunteer from the audience. It takes great skill to play with someone you don't know and even more so to play with someone who doesn't have any improv training that you know of.

I expected that when the scene started, the kid who volunteered would hold back and Jill would take the lead. That did not happen. As soon as they opened, the random audience volunteer fell to the ground and started calling out in a little whiny voice, "You are a terrible mommy! I want to see Daddy."

---

1. Jill Bernard, *Jill Bernard's Small Cute Book of Improv* (YESand.com Publishing, 2012). The book is a little difficult to find so I recommend you start by looking at jillbernard.com.

In the time it took for my eyes to travel from the volunteer to Jill she had already found her character. She was slumped down and slouching like someone who had been beaten down by the world. It was so fast. She mimed a drag off a cigarette and said, "That's fine, but if you want to see your daddy you better get a shovel." It took a second for the audience to catch up. Then we got it. She was the terrible mother the kid said she was and his father was dead and buried. That joke was dark, but it didn't come from just wit. It was the character and delivery that made it. I am still in awe.

Jill's guide to forming a character starts with a small piece of inspiration that you "Yes, &" in yourself as you discover the character that is emerging. She points to five different sources for that inspiration and she calls them "VAPAPO"—Voice, Attitude, Posture, Animal, Prop, and Obsession. If you grab a hold of one of those—say a specific kind of high-pitched voice—the whole character can emerge from it. Voice is probably obvious enough. Start talking in a lower tone and before you know it, you are using the royal "we" and standing as if there was a crown on your head. Attitude means you pick an emotional state. Start off as anxious and before you know it, you are a nuclear physicist who plagiarized his PhD and is now handling real plutonium for the first time. Similarly with posture: tilt your head to one side and before you know it, you are the black sheep of the family at Thanksgiving calling out the dysfunction that no one else sees. Animal, prop, and obsession are a little more advanced, but all work the same way. You make one choice and then the rest of the character flows from there. It is ridiculously helpful, and it turns character work into character play.

Exercise: Character Walk

Find some time and an empty space. Walk around the room. Notice how you walk. Do you lead with a part of your body? Maybe your nose or your feet or your elbows. Find something distinctive about your gait. Once you do, begin to exaggerate that. At first exaggerate a little, then a little more, and so on. Once you get a feel for that, shake it off and return to your normal walk.

Keep walking and choose a different part of your body to lead with. Once again, it could be the elbows or the chin—whatever catches you. As you discover it, begin to exaggerate it. Think about what kind of person walks like that. What else is true about their posture? What does their voice sound like? Try to make the sound of their voice. Do they have a catchphrase? What is their job? Do they like it? What is their family like? Continue to "Yes, &" your choices. It is okay—maybe even good—to be silly. Remember that because you made this character there is something in it that you love.[2] Try to find what you love about this unique character.

Now do that five more times. •

Oh, S—t, I Am a Christian

Everyone is a mystery, especially to ourselves. Some of our character is chosen, some of it is endowed, but most of it is discovered.

I will never forget one of my greatest moments of clarity. I was driving back to work after therapy, and I was thinking about the conversations I had had with my therapist over the previous six months. I was seeing a secular therapist intentionally. There is a lot to say about Christian therapy, both good and bad, but I felt like I needed to go to a secular one. Being a priest is part of my identity, but it can easily take over. A priest can lose touch with themselves without the right balance, so I thought I needed to step away from the churchy things to work out my own stuff. I had been a priest for over seven years, so it was worthwhile to take stock.

---

2. That is an important part of improv. It is also helpful to remember when we try to understand how God, the great Creator, loves us so despite wars, famine, and fashion disasters.

As I was driving and thinking, I realized that in every session I went in planning to talk about something about me, but in order to explain I ended up telling a story about Jesus or something from the Bible or the life of a saint. I wondered why I did that. Why could I not communicate what was going on with me without telling a story about Jesus? As I sat at a stoplight, it hit me like a flash: "Oh, s—t, I am a Christian."

I think it's funny that it took me seven years of ordained ministry to realize that I was in fact a Christian, but what is really telling was my swearing. I knew the Bible. I knew that the people in it gave everything for this pearl of great price. I knew that once you discover the kingdom of heaven nothing else matters. Being a Christian for real, not just as a label, means giving your whole life and your whole self. I had devoted my career to ministry, but in that moment I realized that God had already won my soul too.

This isn't strange, as conversions go. John 3 introduces a religious leader named Nicodemus. He was curious about Jesus but didn't want people to know it. He came to explore in the night. They had a cryptic conversation. After that, Nicodemus disappeared from the gospel story until the surprise ending: Jesus's closest disciples ran away after the crucifixion, and Nicodemus came forward in the daylight to claim Jesus's body. That took guts, faith, and commitment. Nicodemus clearly didn't have those traits when he first met Jesus. He discovered his true character while no one was watching. Like I said, that isn't strange as conversions go. **Transformation is usually only recognized in the rearview mirror.**

But that poses a problem. If transformation is usually only seen in hindsight, how do we do the one big thing that Jesus asked us to do from the top of a mountain after his resurrection (Matt. 28:16–20)? How do we make disciples?

By disciples, I don't just mean people who call themselves Christian. I don't just mean cajoling people into repeating, "Jesus is my Savior, Redeemer, and Lord" on command. I don't just mean people who live according to a certain moral code. I mean, how do we create an environment where people die to the incipient Deism that infects our churches and discover the resurrected power of Jesus alive? By the way, right after Jesus said, "Go therefore and make disciples," he said, "And remember, I am with you always, to the end of the age." That should have been a big hint that discipleship only happens with an ongoing encounter with the divine.

The Church and Metrics

Most pastors and lay leaders today will tell you that the church is in a crisis. We look at falling attendance numbers and scratch our heads as to what they mean. At best, we talk about how people's lives are increasingly complex and how we shouldn't expect people to take an hour every Sunday. At worst, we complain about the lost priorities of a generation. We bemoan how church isn't important enough anymore.

At the same time most caring pastors and truly committed laypeople will give just about anything for their church, which is the problem. Incredibly talented pastors work deep into Saturday night putting together their sermons, an annual report, and three different worship bulletins for the three different congregations they serve so that they can try to make ends meet. Church means stability to most of those committed to it. With declining resources, we literally kill ourselves to try to keep the things we know alive. Plus, we are Christians so the martyr complex just seems natural.

By now you have probably gotten the sense that I vehemently disagree with the core value that says church means stability. The church was born dynamic, mysterious, and unpredictable on Pentecost. It is not wrong for us to want to replicate *the feelings* of the past, but our attempts to insist on doing it the way we did it before are problematic.

Resistance to change is challenging, but there is also another linked problem that is more basic: measurement. We are called to make disciples. But what counts as a disciple? I grew up in the nineties in the heat of the evangelical movement. One of the big strategies then was to put the Christian label on stuff. Kids like skateboarding? Let's call it Christian skateboarding. Kids like concerts? Let's make a concert with music they like with vaguely Christian lyrics. Don't get me wrong. I don't have a problem with praise music. But I remember hearing a joke once that any Christian band could go secular just by changing the "Jesus" to "baby." While I don't think that is completely true,[3] the existence of the joke itself shows how shallow my generation's perception of Christianity is.[4] But the faith in Jesus Christ is all-consuming and transformative. We see that in parable after parable, not to mention in Christian history. I doubt that any of the martyrs would have traded their life for a brand.

Christianity is not just a coat of paint that you slap over life. It isn't just about a word or a high-school clique. **From the outside what I do might seem like two-thousand-year-old cosplay, but discipleship is not about what you think or even what you believe. It is a fundamental shift in how you see the heartbreaking beauty and mystery of our living God's abundant presence, grace, and creativity**.

Every person is a mystery to us, even ourselves. It gets hairy when we try to judge the faith or faithfulness of another. Jesus told us not to try (Matt. 7:1–3). How do we measure a mystery? I don't think we can, but just because we don't have a map doesn't mean we must live without a compass. On the eve of Jesus's death, his disciples were lost and confused; Jesus was trying to give them comfort in his words but it didn't seem to be working. "Do not let your hearts be troubled," he

---

3. There is some deeply meaningful Christian music out there. I can't write an Easter sermon without listening to "Trusty and True" by Damien Rice at least three times.

4. I actually claim no real generation. I am on the cusp of X and Millennial. Some people call us the Oregon Trail generation. I remember the game was super popular, but I would rather watch MacGyver than get dysentery.

told them (John 14:1).[5] Then he said, "Believe in me." He told them that he was leaving, but that there would be a way for them to be united again. Jesus continued by telling the disciples that they would know the way to find him again.

Thomas spoke up for the whole confused class and pled with Jesus, "Lord, we don't know where you are going [or what the heck you are talking about]. How can we know the way?" (John 14:5).

Jesus responded, "I am the way, and the truth, and the life" (John 14:6).

Many people have read that verse to make a case that Christianity is the only way to heaven, but what if Jesus was saying something more profound and even vulnerable? Remember what he had just said: "Do not let your hearts be troubled. Believe in me," and remember who he was talking to. He was in the upper room. He was with his disciples—the people with whom he walked everywhere, shared every meal for three years. They knew who was grumpy at sunrise and who was a morning person. They knew what it was like to joke around and tell stories by the firelight and they knew what Andrew smelled like when he hadn't had a swim in a few days. When Jesus said, "I am the way," what if he was trying to explain to Thomas that the disciples knew the way because they knew Jesus, and so they knew his character? They knew what he was like. They didn't often know what to expect from him, but they knew how to handle him. What if that core of his character was the way, the truth, and the life?

There are countless Christian education programs, Bible studies, and seminaries, but I find it interesting that the original disciples weren't made by a specific course of study. They were made by apprenticeship, by sharing a life together. Aristotle pioneered ethics with the idea that if you want to lead a good life, you should find a

---

5. That worked about as well as a husband telling his wife, "Now don't be angry, but . . ."

good person and hang out with them as much as possible. I can't help but think that is what Jesus was doing.

Churches muse about giving and attendance. Truth be told, even as a priest I don't think I was ever really taught what it means to make a disciple. My priest growing up used to say, "Christianity isn't taught. It is caught." I always took that to mean caught like a virus. If he was right, then most of our programmatic approaches to church are essentially backwards. Maybe becoming a true disciple is not about learning a specific set of things, wearing the right kind of clothes, listening to the right music, and hanging a cross around your neck. It is about finding the character of a true disciple and choosing to play that character until you don't have to think about it anymore. Christianity isn't just about the choices we make; it is about how we train ourselves to respond out of the character that God gives.

No Yardstick

The problem with "personal transformation" or even "discipleship" is that we don't know how to define them, much less measure them. Doubtless you have heard it said, "If you can't measure it, it doesn't exist." That is hogwash. If you can't measure it, we simply haven't found out how to measure it yet. Just because you can't measure something doesn't mean that you can't know things about it. For example, there is a lot of debate about the role of guns in American society. One of the problems with that from an empirical perspective is that because there is no universal gun registry we literally have no idea how many legal, much less illegal guns are out there. There is a number. We just don't have it. Researchers will often use what is called a proxy variable when they can't get the actual number. They use something they *can* measure as a substitute or "proxy" for something they can't measure. We don't know how many guns are on the street, but we do know how many subscriptions there are to gun enthusiast magazines and we surmise if one number goes up so does the other.

Proxy Problems

Without realizing it, churches have been focusing on what statisticians call proxy variables for some time. We don't know how to measure discipleship in our congregations, so we fill in other numbers: average Sunday attendance, giving, or number of giving units. Our thought is that if we can see trends in these things, it will tell us about the thing we really care about. For most of the country, average Sunday attendance is down, but is discipleship? I would argue that we don't know because we have only been going by church attendance or stated affiliation as proxies. But are those accurate?

Take my gun ownership example. Imagine that because of the rise of the internet, magazine subscriptions have tanked across the board. People have access to all kinds of content on their phones and they don't pay for glossy pages anymore. In this reasonably imagined scenario, gun magazine subscriptions would plummet. Does that mean that there are fewer guns on the street? No. It means that there is something going on with the proxy variable that is separate from the number we are looking for.

I am not saying that discipleship is not in crisis. My guess is that it is. What I am saying is that we don't actually know as much as we think we do, because we are looking at proxy variables rather than what we actually care about, which is discipleship.

I don't have a plan for solving the church's metric problem, and even if I did, I don't know that I would care. Faithfulness doesn't depend on success, and according to scripture our pain point has often been our turning point. But I do care about discipleship. That is our mission, right? Even if we don't have metrics for it, you would think we would care more about true discipleship than we do about the number of people with nothing better to do on a Sunday morning.

Accidental Disciples

As I mentioned, I am not sure that I was taught much about making disciples. I don't think anyone is at fault, but I became painfully aware in my ministry that our scriptures and rhetoric talk a lot about discipleship, and while I have learned wonderful things about missional (outward-facing) theology, worship, and church leadership, I haven't really learned much about what it was like to make a disciple. I knew that true disciples existed. Every community I have ever known was blessed with genuinely caring, giving people. Some of them knew their Bible. Some didn't. But all of them in their own way were deeply faithful to God and constantly trying to hold up the best in the people around them.

One of those people in my congregation came to me one day and asked that we start a midweek Bible study during the workday. I remember thinking that there was no way it was going to work in our suburban congregation with precious few retirees. She was a stay-at-home mom with kids who were older. We had tried numerous attempts to reach the moms who work in the home, with little or no success. It seemed like the churches with more resources had that market covered.

In general, I am a "let's try it" kind of leader, especially when it is coming from someone with heft. At the same time, I hate setting my volunteers up to fail. Improv taught me to embrace failure, but it feels different when it is your flock. I worked with her to create something that couldn't fail.

We started a Bible discussion on Friday mornings. We talked about the reading for the upcoming Sunday. I told the group that it was the time I should be talking through the reading anyway, so if no one showed up or one person or ten people did it would all be fine. The structure of the conversation was intentionally loose. We went through three questions.

1. What pops out at you from the text?
2. What do you think this text is trying to teach us or our community?
3. What do you want to take away from this discussion?

I am a big fan of that structure.

While the attendance at that Bible study has always been up and down, I have seen people transformed through it like nothing else. People started coming early to talk about pastoral stuff. I noticed people liked to hang around afterward, so I started ending the sessions by awkwardly saying, "Well, that is a Bible study. You don't have to go, but the program is over, so if you want to, go ahead." Once people spent agendaless time together in a supportive community connected to the scriptures, their souls would sprout one after another. The qualities of generosity, kindness, and patience all started to grow. More and more the group integrated God into how they talked about their life. I saw people find faith and watched as this supportive community nurtured them into disciples. We had several solopreneurs who made a comment about not wanting to go but needing to work after. So I said, "Bring your laptop" and they did. Before you know it, we had a whole coworking group at our church.

I realized that we started sharing not just the Bible, nor just our thoughts. We started sharing our lives. I saw people go from being Christians to actual disciples, and it happened completely by accident.

The more I have thought about this, the more it began to make a bizarre kind of sense to me. If grace is a gift and it is free, then that also means it is both undeserved and unconditional. Most classes and church programs work with an agenda. Agendas are great if you want to get something done, but if you want to transform the soul or change how someone sees, then you have to meet them where they are (yes), and then bring the love and character of Jesus in the relationship (&). If discipleship is about learning facts, we need a curriculum; if it is about changing the heart, we need the free agendaless time where we can reflect, connect, and cultivate the character of a true disciple.

Character Pie

We need a way of understanding the character traits of a true disciple, or at least a way to begin to approach it. In a move that is very congruent with my personal character, I created a whole theory with Excel tables and pie charts only to discover later that a simpler form of the same idea was sitting in the Bible the whole time. I think the journey I took is as important as the destination, so come walk with me through it. I want you to create your own definition of discipleship, compare it with mine, and then we can laugh at ourselves together.

This book has a lot of exercises in it. Hopefully you have been doing them all. If you haven't, I won't judge. I won't even tell the teacher. If there is one exercise to do, it is this one, because it helps us focus and begin to define the ineffable transformation in Christ.

I talked about virtues and apprenticeship earlier. I have been a priest over a dozen years. In that time, I have asked countless people to tell me about their life of faith. Not one of them said they picked up a Bible one day and bam! Fewer than four have talked about meeting God in prayer. All the rest talked about someone—a parent, a friend, a mentor, a Sunday school teacher—that had an impact on them. Apprenticeship is not only the oldest and most biblical model of making disciples. It is the only one we know to have ever worked.

I am going to take you through the exercise that I did to help me define the character traits or endowments essential to true discipleship.

Step 1: Pray. If you have more elaborate methods, go for it. If you are unsure, just say out loud, "Hey, God, could you lead me while I am doing this thing? Help show me what you want me to know?"[6]

---

6. Don't I write awesome prayers! I want to rewrite the whole prayer book like that.

Step 2: Think of three or four people in your life you admire spiritually. These should be people you know personally, not just "know of."[7] You don't necessarily have to know them well, but well enough so that you could say a few things about their individual qualities and personalities. List those people.

Step 3: Now list adjectives or virtues that you associate with each of those people. In improv we call these "endowments," and they are basically the givens of a character. Another way of thinking about it is to list what you admire about those people. It may be the way they are. It may be something they do. If you have two people with the same trait—for example, "generous"—just add "x2" to "generous." If there are three, then "x3" and so on. This is a brainstorm, so don't be afraid to make a long list.

Step 4: Look back at the list and ask yourself about each of the adjectives or virtues: Is this attribute part of being a whole person in Jesus or is it just a quirk of the people you picked? For example, on my list I wrote "wears a pink hat" about a guy I know. That probably isn't an essential thing. Even though the *courage* it takes to wear a pink hat as a man when you live on the streets may be an essential part of discipleship, the pink hat itself is not a necessity. As you cross things off, you might find yourself adding virtues that underline the behavior you admire. That's fine. Create your final list, however many things there are.

When I was young, we played a game called Trivial Pursuit. In that game you would start out with a piece that looked like a pie. As you won each of the required categories, you would get a piece or "wedge" to fill in part of your pie. You weren't done until you filled in all the pieces. Imagine your list of endowments like that. To be a true

---

7. If you have a profound relationship with an author, comedian, or other such personality, you can add them to the list. Just make sure you are balancing it with people you know from real life.

disciple, you need to fill all those wedges to become what we call in my church "full-wheel" disciples.

Now you have your definition of a true disciple. You may fit that description, or you may look at it and realize that you are not the full-wheel disciple that you admire. If you look at that pie and you realize that you don't have all the wedges full, fear not. Remember the point of character work. You find one thing, like a voice or a posture, and then you grow yourself by "yes, &"-ing from there. Each of the pieces of the pie will help lead you to the others.

In case you are curious, you can compare the list you have to mine:

1. Compassionate and giving
2. Has significant Christian friendships
3. A regular practice of prayer (it doesn't have to be formal or daily but does need to be incorporated into regular existence)
4. Ability to receive love
5. Openness and an appreciative outlook
6. An emotional response to God's presence in their life
7. Humility and deep honesty

Feel free to pray again, then compare with mine and amend yours if you like, but remember there is no "right" answer. I don't know better than you on this one. You are making your best understanding of a Christian character and who knows who is right? God, and that is it.

Don't be afraid if you don't feel you have the full wheel yet. When I made this chart, I didn't have #4 at all, and I barely had #2.[8]

As I mentioned before, I did this whole thing, and then I discovered it in the Bible. As it turns out, Paul must have gone through a similar exercise. We can find it in the letter to the Galatians. He was trying to explain how we are free, but that freedom didn't mean go crazy and do whatever without consequences. "Walk by the Spirit," he said (Gal. 5:16, NIV). Once again, Paul pointed to the living, vibrant

---

8. Those may have come together at the same time.

presence of God in the Christian life. But how does one recognize the Spirit's gait? Paul had a list of what he called fruits of the Spirit. We know a life centered in God by the qualities that emerge.

Please don't throw out your list. Your Christian character needs to be authentic and make sense to you. While it was wonderful of the Bible to give us this list, I don't want you to start faking your experience of life. Fruits, virtues, endowments, or whatever you want to call them, these qualities are aspirational to *you* and need to be grounded in *your* experience of God. And your list is just that. The fact that you made the list based on your experience of spiritual people means that you made your list based on how God encounters *you* through them. I include Paul's list, however, because it is worth comparing.

> By contrast, the fruit of the Spirit is love, joy, peace, patience, kindness, generosity, faithfulness, gentleness, and self-control. There is no law against such things. (Gal. 5:22–23)

Make a column with all your character endowments on one side and see how they correspond to the fruits of the Spirit that Paul listed. Here is my example:

My List	Corresponding Fruits
Compassionate and giving	Generosity
Christian friendships	Kindness and joy
Practice of prayer	Faithfulness
Ability to receive love	Love
Openness and appreciative outlook	Gentleness
Emotional response to God in life	Joy and patience
Humility and deep honesty	Self-control and peace

When you have it, write it everywhere. I literally have this list as the wallpaper on every one of my computers. You want your list in front of you every day because it tells you the character that you have chosen to play. It is how you want to train your responses, so that when people see this list on your bathroom mirror they are like, "What is that list? It sounds like you."

Remember the lessons of improv: once you know your character, all the other decisions become easier. I am baffled that from the cross, that dark instrument of torture, Jesus could cry out, "Father, forgive them, for they do not know what they are doing." Jesus has the whole divine nature thing in his back pocket, but for the rest of us, the only way we get close to that is to first choose to be forgiving and then practice all the time. All the time. Practice until our body has muscle memory for the emotion of it. Practice until it is a reaction, not just a response.

This is not normally the way we are taught to think about life. We are taught to hate those who hate us and curse those who curse us, but Jesus's way assumes that no one can surrender your character but you. Being a Christian means a lot of things, and one of them is that we surrender the ability to use someone else's dysfunction as a reason to abandon our own integrity. This to me is why the improv practice of taking a character and holding on to it is so important. **Whatever comes to test your character is really a gift for you to show it.**

My Unfunny Joke

If Paul is right, those very same fruits of the spirit should be the Church's ongoing legacy. But, as I mentioned before, we can get stuck in what we have done rather than why we have been doing it.

Years ago, I wrote a joke to explain this problem to myself. Well, I called it a joke, but I must confess it isn't funny. Maybe it is a parable; I will let you decide. For context I wrote it when I was in college and attending an Episcopal Church in Colonial Williamsburg. The area around the church is basically a living history museum with actors who pretend to be from the colonial period. You can go to an old-school pub or attend a witch trial. And most places are called "shoppe." The entire enterprise was the brainchild of a rector of this historic church who got the Rockefeller family to contribute the money to get it going. It is quaint and lovely and it highlights how much of our church traditions are not just rooted in the past but stuck in it. The joke goes like this:

> How many Episcopalians does it take to change a light bulb?
> Change a light bulb? Do you realize that bulb has been there since they invented electricity?!

I told you it wasn't funny. But I tell it to myself often because it is easy for us to honor the past and miss the point of it. **Tradition isn't a light bulb. It is light that shines from it. Stewarding tradition requires changing the bulb.** There is nothing more contrary to the gospel than for the children of the light to sit in darkness because of a misguided notion that it is what God wants.

R.A.T Groups

Hopefully by now you are on board with me. Virtues, qualities, or endowments are the way we should think about our aim as a church rather than the proxy variables of attendance or budget or even our adherence to tradition in the sense of the burned-out bulb. I don't know how we will measure the light. How do you measure transformation? But at the very least, we need to know the difference between our aim and our proxy.

In the midst of your character work, please don't forget the lessons from section II. It is a playful, supportive, and adaptive community that allows Christian virtues to thrive and expand. The disciples of the Bible were made when they lived, ate, walked, laughed, cried, fetched water, and kvetched about the weather all with Jesus at their side. Improv troupes reach true excellence when they know each other as well offstage as they do onstage. Some of my colleagues and I have a theory that the only way to make a disciple is to have someone spend a ridiculous amount of time with other disciples.[9] Within a congregation, even when there are no formal small groups, there are always informal ones. I call these "R.A.T. groups" because they do spend a Ridiculous Amount of Time together. These are deep friends that bear each other's burdens, prayers, and celebrations. Creating or facilitating those relationships is something I wish I knew more about, and in many ways this book is my attempt to try to organize the qualities and strategies of the kind of life and community which create them.

---

9. Thank you to the Rev. Sean Steele and the Rev. Becky Zartman for being conversation partners with me on this. "Ridiculous Amounts of Time" is actually Sean's phrase.

CONCLUSION

This book was written during the COVID-19 pandemic. I believe that the pandemic itself has revealed the need for the integration of improv and ministry more powerfully than I could ever have imagined.

When the pandemic hit, we had to close in-person worship. Since I was a child, I would hum to myself, "Here is the church, here is the steeple, open it up . . ." but when the people can't enter the building without putting their beloved community at risk, then the end of that nursery rhyme becomes haunting. I remember trying to imagine what worship would look like online and I found a video of a church I had once attended. I wanted to see what they were doing. Watching them try to do the exact same service in an empty room to what was obviously a cell phone connected to Facebook Live made me tear up more than a little. I don't think I had it on for more than a minute before I closed the app.

I think the pandemic showed the true colors of many of our churches and church leaders—so many refusing to say "yes" even to figuring out a reality we could share, but also so many miracles.

It was there, amid disaster, that I realized how important adaptive faith really is. All of a sudden, these practices of "Yes, &" became apparent in the life of our community. While I would hear other pastors go on about trying to keep worship looking the same online, we went the other way. We knew that if it looked the same on a screen, it wouldn't feel the same. In a true "Yes, &" moment, I looked at myself in the mirror and I said, "Les, you are no longer the rector of a medium-sized church. You are a digital church planter." Then I added, "With one heck of a prospect list." See the "Yes," and the "&" in that?

Sure enough, our ministry changed, but also found new beauty. At first we didn't know how to patch in music to the services, and we didn't want to put anyone at risk by being in the same room. I play decent guitar, but I chose something else. I stole my five-year-old son's blue ukulele and taught myself how to play it. I felt like with everything stripped down, our music needed to sound innocent and childlike more than it needed to be precise and professional. I would invite people to share welcome notes in the comments and they flooded in. One older member even posted a picture of himself dressed up with a tag that said "usher" on it. I told people to make sure to ask Larry if they needed to find the bathroom.

Before the pandemic, we had made new name tags that included the person's picture on them. I hung them from ribbon on the altar to make a backdrop and I would pray over them every week. People found out and started requesting name tags when they hadn't bothered the first time. They just wanted to feel connected to the life of prayer at the church during that time. COVID has had so many costs, but it became interesting to me how it also made people more aware of their spiritual needs and how God was "Yes, &"-ing the longing of our people.

This became powerfully clear on Palm Sunday. Usually on Palm Sunday we have a blessing of the palm leaves, a walk around the church, and then people can take their palms with them. Not only did we not have people coming, our diocese was clear that they didn't want us distributing the palms because we didn't know the health risks at the time. I was in the church, alone with two hundred preordered palm leaves and no one to give them to. One of the things I have learned about worship is that if things get shaken, go deeper. As I sat there surrounded by foliage, I found something. It occurred to me that we have been doing Palm Sunday backwards.

I had heard other church leaders poke at the churches who wanted to distribute palm leaves, accusing them of being individualistic (wanting "my palm"). I didn't share that view, but I thought about it. In the story of Palm Sunday, the people spread leaves, branches, and cloaks along the way for Jesus. We always take the palms from church, but in the story, it is not about what you get, it is about what you leave. Moreover, those very same people cheering for Jesus's triumphal entry into Jerusalem would be screaming, "Crucify him!" in less than a week. I thought about the palm leaves, and how in other years I have noticed how quickly they wither. I came to think of those leaves as our best and yet failed intentions.

After I explained those thoughts during the sermon, I invited people to share in the comments what good intentions they had that were failing now in the pandemic. As they wrote, I read them aloud, then dropped a palm leaf in the aisle on the way to the altar. It was heartbreaking and beautiful. One teenager wrote, "I had planned to shop for a prom dress with my mom." The palm leaf hit the ground. Another person wrote, "We were going to visit our new grandbaby." Another leaf. A senior in high school wrote, "I was going to go to my graduation." Another leaf. More and more comments flooded in until all the leaves were left on the ground. I have never experienced a Palm Sunday so powerful, and nothing went like it was supposed to, thank God.

Our online ministries opened us up to a level of prayer we had never seen before in church. I always leave space in the service for people to say their prayers out loud, but no one ever does. However, after that day everything changed online. As part of every service, I read the prayers that people posted. I thought because the service was online I should keep it short, so I planned it to last twenty minutes. We never had an online Sunday service less than an hour, just because of the prayers.

Now I see all of Holy Week differently. Jesus walked straight into all the things that in our finitude we fear over and obsess about. His example teaches us that we fear the wrong things. His example shows us that there is something worse than pain, rejection, betrayal, or even death. **Even worse than death is the obsessive need to cling to the withered palms of yesterday's blessings**. Because when we do, our arms are too full to embrace the mysterious resurrection that is so, so close.

This adventure is the path of true discipleship. Don't worry if it is scary. Every one of the disciples ran away until they could find enough trust to step back in. The best things in life are awkward and the empty tomb is no exception. In these pages I hope you found a taste of what I did at that high school retreat when the deacon wrapped his stole around the girl proclaiming the gospel. I pray you have, because each of us stands like that girl at the Gospel Book, struggling to let our life preach what grace is like. If you need permission or a stole to wrap around your shoulders, you are welcome to mine. But I urge you to speak, discover, and learn the awkwardly beautiful lesson of the gospel. Everything you have been taught is untrue. Life isn't short. Death is short. Life is forever.

Think about that: all that we do to hide from death and loss. All the hurts we absorb and recycle. And none of it really matters. Christ's Love is life's spring, and it will flow forever despite our awkward anxiety. God took the cross, the most brutal method of torture and death in history, and "Yes, &"-ed it all the way to the ultimate symbol of love and life eternal.

When you get it, you see that it is truly, beautifully hilarious.

Easter is the best punchline ever.

No joke.

Welcome to the very select group of Christians who can hear that cosmic punchline and laugh. Welcome to the endgame of this agendaless book. Welcome to the group of Christians who harness the power of play and radical acceptance, and find the courage to risk looking like idiots. Together we can do so much more good, create so much more change, and learn so much more about Jesus's character than anyone practicing the strategies stolen from a seminary bookshelf. In my introduction I told you that I used to wonder about what kind of person would get the idea to both preserve church tradition and empower that young woman by wrapping the stole around her shoulder. Congratulations, now you are that kind of person.

As my friend, the Rev. Gini Gerbasi says, "Good luck with that."

APPENDIX

Les's Rules for Conversational Sermons

1. **Get to a question fast**. You want the congregation to see that you are most interested in what they have to say. The most common mistake a facilitator can make is to "front load" the conversation with his or her thoughts. Hold on to what you have to say about the passage. You will need it later.

2. **Ask open-ended questions**. If you want to ask a question with a specific answer, stop yourself. Just make the point as a comment. People want to hear what you have to say. They don't want to feel like you are testing them.

3. **Listen!** It is your curiosity that will give the sermon energy, and the people can tell if you care what they have to say or not.

4. **Take congregant's thoughts to the next level.** As the facilitator, you are looking to deepen the level of conversation and provide resources from the Christian tradition. It is good to have the types of points you would make in a morning sermon in your back pocket and then look for when the congregation sets the stage for those points. "Yes, &" is your best friend.

5. **Affirm, or at least clarify.** If someone rambles, feel free to focus on the one thing that they said that you think is of value. "One thing you said that I really liked was . . ." If someone makes a point and you want to make the opposite, then something like the phrase, "Yes, and I wonder" is probably a lot more

helpful than simply saying "But..." If someone says something that you don't want associated with the community's position, then simply summarize, "So you think that..., interesting."

6. **Ask for help if you need it**. If you don't understand what someone is trying to say, feel free to ask them to explain more. That shows you care what they have to say. After you summarize, it is good to check to see if you understood correctly. "Did I have that right?" If someone asks a question or opens a door that you don't know how to deal with, feel free to ask the congregation as a whole to talk about the topic. "I'm not sure, what do the rest of you think?"

ACKNOWLEDGMENTS

I want to thank Joni and Jason Buck for providing their rental home as a writer's retreat. It is called the Grand Victorian in Galveston, Texas. You should stay there. It is awesome.

I want to give a shout-out to all my improv teachers, especially those from ComedySportz Indianapolis, who taught me to love this art. My heartfelt gratitude for my improv partner and friend, Carrie Koch. Your passion and skill for improv is an inspiration. And your compassion and talent for applied improv is unmatched. Thank you for playing through most of these ideas when they were still in their infancy.

I also want to thank my Friday morning Bible crew and my friends from Shaka Power Yoga who always give enthusiastic encouragement.

My deep gratitude goes to the leaders, staff, and people of St. Aidan's. Their gracefulness and generosity are an inspiration, not to mention the fact that they put up with my incessant strings of puns. I also want to thank Church Publishing for reaching out to me to write this book.

No thanks will ever be enough to Kristin for being an incredible mother to our kids and partner to me while giving me the space to work on all this stuff. So I guess I will just give James and Sam the biggest hugs and then unload the dishes.

I also want to thank my friend Becky. Without her encouragement and support, I never could have even started this book, and now I am finished.